A

TASTE of HEAVEN

JEREMY P. TARCHER/PENGUIN

a member of Penguin Group (USA) Inc.

New York

A
TASTE of HEAVEN

A GUIDE TO FOOD AND DRINK MADE BY MONKS AND NUNS

Madeline Scherb

JEREMY P. TARCHER/PENGUIN
Published by the Penguin Group
Penguin Group (USA) Inc., 375 Hudson Street, New York, New York 10014, USA •
Penguin Group (Canada), 90 Eglinton Avenue East, Suite 700, Toronto, Ontario M4P 2Y3, Canada
(a division of Pearson Canada Inc.) • Penguin Books Ltd, 80 Strand, London WC2R 0RL, England • Penguin Ireland,
25 St Stephen's Green, Dublin 2, Ireland (a division of Penguin Books Ltd) • Penguin Group (Australia),
250 Camberwell Road, Camberwell, Victoria 3124, Australia (a division of Pearson Australia Group Pty Ltd) •
Penguin Books India Pvt Ltd, 11 Community Centre, Panchsheel Park, New Delhi–110 017, India •
Penguin Group (NZ), 67 Apollo Drive, Rosedale, North Shore 0632, New Zealand
(a division of Pearson New Zealand Ltd) • Penguin Books (South Africa) (Pty) Ltd,
24 Sturdee Avenue, Rosebank, Johannesburg 2196, South Africa

Penguin Books Ltd, Registered Offices: 80 Strand, London WC2R 0RL, England

Most Tarcher/Penguin books are available at special quantity discounts for bulk purchase for sales promotions,
premiums, fund-raising, and educational needs. Special books or book excerpts also can be created to fit specific needs.
For details, write Penguin Group (USA) Inc. Special Markets, 375 Hudson Street, New York, NY 10014.

Library of Congress Cataloging-in-Publication Data

Scherb, Madeline.
A taste of heaven : a guide to food and drink made by monks and nuns / Madeline Scherb.
p.   cm.
ISBN 978-1-58542-718-5
1. Cookery, International.   2. Alcoholic beverages.   3. Monastic and religious life.   I. Title.
TX725.A1S4154   2009   2009017625
641.59—dc22

Printed in the United States of America
1   3   5   7   9   10   8   6   4   2

BOOK DESIGN BY NICOLE LAROCHE

The recipes contained in this book are to be followed exactly as written. The publisher is not responsible for specific health or allergy needs that may require medical supervision. The publisher is not responsible for any adverse reactions to the recipes contained in this book.

While the author has made every effort to provide accurate telephone numbers and Internet addresses at the time of publication, neither the publisher nor the author assumes any responsibility for errors, or for changes that occur after publication. Further, the publisher does not have any control over and does not assume any responsibility for author or third-party websites or their content.

For my parents, Frank and Margarita Scherb,
and in loving memory of Brother Raphael Prendergast, OCSO,
Abbey of Gethsemani

CONTENTS

FOREWORD

They are truly monks when they live by the labor of their hands, as did our fathers and the apostles.

—RULE OF SAINT BENEDICT, CHAPTER 48

Food should be treated with respect since Our Lord left himself to us in the guise of food.

—DOROTHY DAY

The early monks supported themselves by the work of their hands, usually weaving mats, hats, rugs, baskets, and other products that they later sold at nearby local markets. Work is an integral part of all human life, be it inside or outside a monastery. Therefore, monks seriously apply themselves to the humble task of earning their living, not wishing to beg or be a burden to anyone.

What differentiates the monk's approach to work from that of others is the attitude he brings to it. Monastic work is functional. It is not motivated by a desire for a career or for success, and even less by greed. The first function of monastic work is that it be in the imitation of Jesus and Saint Joseph, the humble carpenters of Nazareth. Along with Mary, they give us an example of how to live and order the pattern of our lives. The second function of monastic work is to provide for the monastery and those who inhabit it. The third important aspect of all monastic work is the element of balance that work brings to the daily rhythm of monastic life.

A *Taste of Heaven* is the result of a personal monastic pilgrimage. It gives the reader a glimpse into the unique life of some of the most remote monasteries of both Europe and the United States. The book tells the tale of the histories, practices, and artisanal products of these monasteries and explores the stories of the monks and nuns who live, work, and worship within their walls. It reads like a virtual tour of these places of profound silence. Its pages, filled with gentle anecdotes particular to each monastery or monastic figure, should be read quietly, as a form of guided meditation.

The author also does all of us a great service by making available an exquisite collection of recipes derived from various monasteries. These recipes have as their source the many different products traditionally made by monks and nuns: cheese, ales, wines, liqueurs, olive oil, chocolates, vinegars, tapenades, herbs, candies, and baked goods. In following these recipes and making use of these products, we discover the secret character of monastic cookery: a cuisine known for its simplicity, sobriety, and basic good taste. Individuals such as the author who have partaken in the gracious hospitality of the monasteries mentioned in this book can attest to the healthy, balanced diet practiced by monks and nuns. In most cases the food presented at the monastery table consists of products from the monastery farms and gardens, coupled with local produce prepared with a great deal of love and presented with simplicity. Such simplicity need not preclude elegance; in fact, monks and nuns believe that simplicity itself is synonymous with elegance.

I trust the reader will be inspired by the beautiful stories in this book to discover the products made not only by the monasteries mentioned here, but also by those monasteries located closer to their homes. Many monasteries, including ours, sell their products at local farmers' markets or at annual festivals, such as our Summer Vinegar Festival and Christmas Fair. People appreciate having these products made readily available to them. These days they can even be purchased online. Whatever the case, the reader contributes directly to the livelihood of monasteries by appreciating and purchasing their products. May this always be, so that, in Saint Benedict's words, "God may be glorified in all things."

BROTHER VICTOR-ANTOINE D'AVILA-LATOURRETTE

November 13, 2008

Feast of All Monastic Saints

La Grangeville, New York

INTRODUCTION

Bells are the heartbeat of abbey life. They call the community to prayer throughout the day. They can be loud or soft, joyful or soulful. A new bell becomes part of the monastic family in a kind of bell baptism: it is blessed and is sometimes named after a saint. When the monks of Stift Heiligenkreuz in Austria recently climbed the pop charts with their recordings of chant, they even included the abbey's bells in between songs.

However, a guest who stays at an abbey overnight may feel something other than love for the bell that tolls around three a.m. for Vigils, the first prayer service of the day. This is especially true at Gethsemani Abbey in Kentucky, where the formidable bell can make a bleary-eyed guest feel like one has been tied to the clapper in a plot invented by Charlie Chaplin.

Some monastery guests have trouble getting up for Vigils, but the monks and nuns are used to it. Many of them describe Vigils as a peaceful way to begin the day and to prepare for work. Perhaps that's why food made by monks and nuns tastes heavenly. Another likely reason is that the balance between prayer and work at a monastery is, as one French monk enthusiastically puts it, *"merveilleux, merveilleux!"* Simply marvelous. Monks and nuns live to pray, not to work.

Meanwhile, at three a.m. in the secular world most people are still fast asleep. Their day holds little promise of prayer or song, unless the former is for a raise and the latter occurs in the shower. It's difficult to find balance on any given day, and all too often people feel like they live to work.

What can the rest of us learn from the way monks and nuns live and the exceptional products they make? It isn't just that they pray seven times a day, prefer silence, and shun TV (all things that secular folks can also do), or that they choose to serve God in a monastic community rather than raise a family. Their life is also defined by a specific rule of conduct. One of the earliest monastic rules was the Rule of Saint Benedict, written in the sixth century. Prayer, work, and spiritual reading remain the pillars of Benedictine monastic life to this day.

Benedict places importance on singing the Divine Office above all else but also instructs monks to work, saying, "He who lives by the work of his own hands is truly a monk." (The famous Abbey of Cîteaux prints a variation on Benedict's dictum, *Prière & Travail*—prayer and work—on the label of its eponymous cheese.) Manual labor is important for monks not only because they are following in the footsteps of the Apostles and Jesus, who was a carpenter, but also because Benedict warns that idleness is the enemy of the soul.

Monks and nuns must earn enough to sustain their abbeys, but they never strive to make money for money's sake. They are also immune from the constant pressure to make shareholders richer. When the monks at Westmalle Abbey recently chose to cap production of their world-renowned beer despite increasing demand, they made a decision that was as unlikely in corporate America as it would be for an incompetent manager to confess his faults. Monks and nuns work just enough to support their monasteries while some, such as Westmalle, use surplus profits for charity.

The work that monks and nuns do is intertwined with the monastic way of life; one can't be separated from the other. Monks and nuns see the earth as God's creation and each living thing as part of that creation. They see God's love for us in the beauty of this creation rather than in manmade things—the fancy homes, luxury cars, expensive clothes, fame, and fortune that some folks crave. When they rise for prayer before dawn they are participating in God's creation. When they sing the Psalms they are doing the same. When they make caramels, cheese, beer, chocolate, jam, and other marvelous foods, they are creating something special that makes the world a better place. Their work is essentially a form of sharing God's love with the rest of us.

How lucky we are! It's impossible not to taste the love with which these foods are made when one bites into a silky-smooth, buttery vanilla caramel from Mississippi Abbey in Iowa or gets a whiff of beer served fresh from the Orval brewery in Belgium. As caretakers of God's creation, monks and nuns have always been inclined to use what are now called organic ingredients. Whenever possible, monastery products are made with fresh, locally sourced ingredients such as butter, milk, wholesome grains, hops, and grapes, and rarely use preservatives. (Fruitcake being fruitcake, even some monastic recipes call for artificial colors and flavors, but it's still a treat.)

Monks and nuns have been making food for more than a thousand years. They used to make foods like cheese, bread, wine, and beer for their own consumption and sold the surplus to travelers and pilgrims. Occasionally food would be served to a special guest like the Emperor Charlemagne, who is thought to have discovered Roquefort cheese at an abbey.

All of the monastic communities in this book are wholly contemplative, meaning that they exist to pray rather than to teach in schools or work in hospitals, yet they must be self-sufficient. Most of them farmed crops until it became either too labor-intensive or unprofitable. When they looked for other ways to support themselves, many turned to making other kinds of food for sale.

Some foods that need time to mature, such as cheese, beer, wine, and fruitcake, are easier to make than other products, given the monastic schedule. Other treats, like chocolate and caramels, are quite labor intensive but still fit nicely into the monastic day. Some monasteries (especially the ones that make candy) are run like small family-owned businesses, while others such as Chimay and Westmalle in Belgium own large breweries and employ lay workers. (Look for the Authentic Trappist Product label on the bottle to be sure a beer is made entirely on the grounds of an abbey; many beers known as "abbey ales" are not made at or by monasteries.)

Today heavenly foods are being made at monasteries around the world, including more than one hundred monasteries in France alone. Many of them are experts in their craft, such as Bonneval in the Midi-Pyrénées, which is the only European abbey that makes chocolate from scratch. Some monasteries inherited recipes from laypersons—for cheesecake, candy, and homeopathic elixirs, to name a few—while others have invented their own. Newer monastic foundations in Africa and Latin America make world-class coffee, cheese, and other delicacies. Wherever they are made, monastery foods taste heavenly!

Perhaps the greatest lesson to be learned from the example of monks and nuns is that a life lived simply can be both rewarding and sustainable. As mentioned above, monks and nuns don't live to work, they live to pray. They work only as much as they need to, but they give it their best effort every day. They work whether they are young or old, according to their abilities (an octogenarian nun was recently spotted making chocolates at Bonneval, while monks of a similar age staff the reception desk at Gethsemani).

A monastery's environmental footprint is humble. Many monks and nuns (all those who follow Saint Benedict's rule) are vegetarian. Some abbeys in the United States and Europe have donated land to create wildlife preserves, while others like Guadalupe and Saint Joseph's are certified "green" foresters. As the Buddhist monk Thich Nhat Hanh might say, monks and nuns tread gently upon the earth. It's an example the rest of us would do well to follow. If you want to visit a monastery, start with one that is nearby to cut down on the environmental impact of your visit; better yet, get there by train or bike (this is not always possible, as many monasteries are purposefully placed in the middle of nowhere). It's also easy to sample monastery products by shopping online (see the Shopping Guide, page 199).

Perhaps the best way to taste food made by monks and nuns is to share it with someone you love. Saint Benedict says to welcome guests as though they were Christ. Why not invite someone over and cook a meal made with monastery ingredients, sip a hearty Trappist ale or a lovely Riesling from Saint Hildegard, and serve a slice of nuns' cheesecake with a plate of monastery chocolates for dessert? This is a simple act of creation and hospitality that any of us can manage no matter what our cooking skills may be. Saint Benedict would be pleased.

CELESTIAL SPIRITS

Beer is proof that God loves us and wants us to be happy.

—BENJAMIN FRANKLIN

There's a famous story about Saint Benedict that has all the makings of a sitcom—monks behaving badly try to poison their abbot but are thwarted by a miracle. The background story would go something like this: It is the sixth century, and monasticism has taken root in the West. As there is still no agreement on formal rules of behavior, some monks prefer to make up their own. One such group of monks invites Saint Benedict to be their abbot, but when he writes a strict new rule of conduct they begin to regret their choice. They ponder how easy it would be to go back to their lazy, selfish ways if only they could get rid of the pesky new abbot—so they offer him a cup of poisoned wine.

We know that this much of the story is true, and the rest is legend: When offered the wine, Benedict made the sign of the cross, and the cup shattered.

It's ironic that monks would use wine in a murder plot. Wine is many things to Christians—a symbol of Christ's sacrifice, a reminder of the Last Supper, an important part of Mass—but rarely a murder weapon. Of course, most monks throughout the ages have used wine for peaceful purposes. In the Middle Ages monasteries each had a little *clos*, an enclosed vineyard, where the monks made wine for Mass and for their own consumption. Extra wine was sold or served to guests, as it still is today.

Monasteries were repositories for all kinds of knowledge in the Middle Ages, from the writings of ancient authors to herbal remedies to viticulture. Monks and nuns made significant contributions to advancing our knowledge of the natural world. Saint Martin is said to have invented a pruning method that is still used in vineyards today, Dom Pérignon perfected the art of blending grapes to make Champagne at the Abbey of Hautevillers, and before the French Revolution, monasteries owned some of the world's most famous vineyards, such as Clos Romanée. And in a fortunate act of serendipity, the monks who hid wine from invading barbarians by storing it in abbey cellars also invented some of Europe's best early wine vaults.

One thing roving barbarians and monks had in common in northern climates was a preference for beer over wine. Like wine, beer was safer than most sources of drinking water. Monks were also allowed to consume beer during Lent, when it served as a kind of "liquid bread." Monks at some abbeys could drink up to five liters of beer a day! Abbeys first began making beer for their own consumption; extra beer was served in the monastery pubs that were common along pilgrim routes or to guests, as it still is today.

The fifteenth century ushered in the Protestant Reformation, along with the curious notion that Mass could be said without wine. The French Revolution followed in the eighteenth century, and many abbeys were razed to the ground (including the great abbey where Saint Martin had preached). Monks and nuns returned to France after the Revolution, but secular producers had usurped some monastic traditions—the art of making Champagne, for one—and many monasteries now turned to making cheese or liqueurs to survive.

Carthusian monks make Chartreuse, the only liqueur in the world that can boast of being both a popular digestive in France and an occasional farmer's aid for flatulent cows. Chartreuse matures in the world's largest liqueur-aging cave, in nearby Voiron, where visitors can sample the green and yellow versions of the elixir. The best way to learn more about this order and its unique spiritual contribution to monasticism is to watch the documentary *Into Great Silence*, or read *An Infinity of Little Hours*, the true tale of several young men who chose to explore a Carthusian vocation.

Liqueurs are part of a broader tradition of monastic elixirs, some of which contained alcohol and some of which did not. Benedictine liqueur, no longer made by monks, is based on a monastic recipe. The medieval monks at Orval Abbey sold a tonic called Orval water, which contained water from the abbey's well with a few other secret ingredients and was said to have curative powers (as was Chartreuse). The monks of Aiguebelle in the Drôme Provençale still make a tasty plant-based elixir that is free of alcohol and surprisingly refreshing; it's worth seeking out the abbey for its elixir as well as its stunning beauty, lovely guesthouse, and proximity to Montélimar, the nougat capital of France. In Portugal, monks at the Monastery of Singeverga have resisted the trend toward commissioned products and still make a very sweet liqueur, which can be sipped by guests on retreat.

Monks and nuns continue to make wine, beer, liqueurs, and even bourbon-soaked fruitcakes and fudge. The Trappist monks in Belgium make famous beer, and an American monastery in New Mexico has experimented with brewing. Saint Benedict himself says in his rule that he was unable to convince his monks to give up wine, so he recommends that it be drunk in moderation or not at all by those with the fortitude to abstain. So pick your drink of choice—be it elixir, liqueur, wine, or beer—and raise a toast to the monasteries!

It could be the stuff of a James Bond movie. Take one ancient order of monks who are especially reclusive, add a secret liqueur recipe that is known to only two monks in the entire world, and throw in a high-tech computer system that allows the monks to control distillation in a nearby town without leaving the monastery, and voilà! Welcome to the world of Chartreuse.

The monks got their secret recipe for Chartreuse from a Frenchman in the seventeenth century, but it was confiscated during the French Revolution. The French bureaucrats couldn't decipher the recipe and eventually gave it back.

Chartreuse is made with 130 herbs that are carefully selected and prepared by the monks at the monastery before being sent to the Chartreuse distillery in Voiron, where the liqueur is distilled and aged in oak casks. Visitors to the distillery can tour the world's largest liqueur cellar, see a 3-D movie of the monks gathering herbs in the mountains, and sample Chartreuse in the tasting room. In addition to Chartreuse, the gift shop sells berry-flavored liqueurs, hard candies in herbal flavors like gentian, and reproductions of the double-handled Carthusian mugs that the monks use in their cells (the double handles remind the monks that they never act alone, and that God provides for them in every way, including food and drink).

The Grande Chartreuse monastery is a short drive from Voiron, and while it is not open to visitors, one of the buildings on the grounds has been converted into a museum and gift shop. If one comes to the monastery to visit the museum and happens to pass a pair of Carthusians out for their weeky walk (this is the only time they leave the monastic enclosure), simply say *"Bonjour."* Otherwise, practice silence here to get a glimpse of what it might have felt like nine hundred years ago, when Saint Bruno led his fellow hermits up the mountain to found this holy place.

Chartreuse isn't only for drinking. Charles de Gaulle was fond of Chartreuse-filled chocolates, and the liqueur is surprisingly versatile in cooking. Here are some recipes from the Chartreuse distillery.

CHRISTMAS COCOA

1 cup hot chocolate

1 part green Chartreuse

Whipped cream (optional)

Brew one cup of hot chocolate. Stir in Chartreuse and top with fresh whipped cream. Serve immediately.

ORANGE SUNBURST

3 parts orange juice

1 part green Chartreuse

Fill a cocktail shaker with ice. Add Chartreuse and orange juice and shake well. Serve over ice.

Abbot's Elixir

1 part yellow Chartreuse

1 glass very cold extra-dry Champagne

Add Chartreuse to Champagne and swirl glass gently to combine. Serve immediately.

Monk's Tonic

1 part green Chartreuse

9 parts tonic water

Fill a cocktail shaker with ice. Add tonic water and Chartreuse and shake well. Serve over ice.

1 pound peeled and deveined jumbo tiger shrimp, tail on (optional), patted dry

Salt and freshly ground white pepper

1½ tablespoons unsalted butter

2 tablespoons orange juice

2 scallions, greens only, finely chopped, plus sliced scallions for garnish

2 tablespoons green Chartreuse, slightly warmed

1. Generously season the shrimp with salt and pepper. Melt the butter in a large skillet over medium-high heat. When the butter is bubbling, add the shrimp and sauté until cooked through, 4 to 5 minutes.

2. Add the orange juice and reduce the heat to low. Cook another minute, then stir in the scallion greens. Remove the pan from the heat, add the Chartreuse, then light by either tipping the pan slightly toward the flame of the burner or using a long match. Let the flame go out on its own.

3. Transfer the shrimp to a platter, garnish with sliced scallion, and serve immediately.

2 tablespoons unsalted butter

2 slices thick-sliced bacon, cut crosswise into ¼-inch strips

5 shallots, finely chopped

3 boneless skinless chicken breasts, each cut crosswise into 4 thick pieces

Salt and freshly ground black pepper

¼ cup dry white wine

8 ounces mushrooms, cleaned and sliced

2 tablespoons green Chartreuse

¼ cup crème fraîche

1 tablespoon chopped fresh tarragon

4 cups cooked white rice

1 tablespoon finely chopped fresh parsley

1. Melt the butter in a 12-inch heavy skillet over medium-high heat. Add the bacon and shallots and sauté for 3 minutes. Transfer the bacon and shallots to a small bowl with a slotted spoon, leaving the butter in the pan.

2. Increase the heat to medium-high. Generously season the chicken with salt and pepper, then add the chicken to the pan with the butter and lightly brown on both sides. Add the wine and deglaze, scraping up the browned bits from the bottom of the pan. Add the mushrooms and return the bacon and shallots to the pan. Stir to mix well. Reduce the heat to medium-low, add the Chartreuse, and partially cover. Simmer until the chicken is cooked through, 3 to 5 minutes.

3. Stir in the crème fraîche and fresh tarragon and adjust the seasonings. Serve on a bed of fluffy white rice and garnish with the parsley.

SINGEVERGA MONASTERY (MOSTEIRO DE SINGEVERGA)

WWW.MOSTEIRODESINGEVERGA.COM

Portugal is a food lover's paradise, but surprisingly few foodies have discovered Singeverga liqueur, a sweet liqueur made by the monks of Singeverga Monastery in the district of Porto.

The monks' eponymous liqueur is famous among locals, who use it to flavor king cake (*bolo rei*), Portugal's renowned Christmas cake. King cake is a ring-shaped sweet bread that traditionally contains a hidden fava bean (whoever finds the bean either hosts the next Christmas party or bakes the next king cake). Sadly, as the monks are not yet licensed to export Singeverga, anyone unable to travel to the monastery can only imagine how good a king cake can be when made with this liqueur, whose delicious blend of spices includes cinnamon, saffron, nutmeg, cloves, coriander, calamus, and angelica root.

These are the only Benedictine monks in Portugal today. There were once many Benedictine monasteries here, but they were all suppressed in the early nineteenth century. The first monastery to be restored (by monks from Brazil, in 1875) was Cucujães, which in turn founded Singeverga in 1892; when Cucujães closed, the monks at Singeverga were the only ones left standing.

The monastery feels unusually new, as the current buildings date only to 1955, but it's still picturesque with its red tile roofs and lovely cloister. Men and women are welcome for retreats.

HOW TO ENJOY A TRAPPIST BEER

A well-known British TV chef once wrote a best-selling cookbook that featured a two-page description of how to boil an egg. On the same principle, we asked Tim Webb—one of Britain's best-known beer writers and author of *Good Beer Guide: Belgium* (www.booksaboutbeer.com)—to tell readers how to pour a beer properly.

FIRST, SOURCE YOUR BEER.

Trappist beers are all living products. They are bottled with yeast, which continues to mature and develop the beer's flavor in the bottle, up to a point when it will then "turn" and become sour, skunky, or otherwise unpleasant.

Living beers do not like to be kept for long periods much below 37°F or above 68°F, so find a beer store with a track record that suggests it buys its beers from reliable importers and distributors.

Bottles need to be treated with similar respect once you bring them home. The perfect cellar temperature is between 46°F and 54°F. There is no need to obsess about humidity. Avoid refrigeration usually and direct sunlight always. Store the beer upright.

BEERS AGE WITH VARYING DEGREES OF GRACEFULNESS.

Stronger beers (8 percent alcohol by volume and above) age better because alcohol is a preservative. Darker beers improve more than paler ones. Larger bottles (24 ounces and above) aid flavor development.

The Trappist beers that keep best in the cellar are Achel Extra Bruin (9.5 percent), Chimay Grand Reserve (9 percent), Rochefort 10 (11.2 percent), Westmalle Tripel (9.5 percent), and Westvleteren Extra 8 (8 percent) and Westvleteren 12

(10.2 percent). Three years' aging is rarely a problem for these brews, and many bottles age reverently for a decade or more.

Trappist beers of lesser strength are usually best enjoyed within a year of production.

HOW TO SERVE TRAPPIST BEER

The best serving temperature for any fine ale is 50° to 54°F—the historical meaning of "room temperature." This allows for a little warming while it is being enjoyed, with the full array of flavor components in an ale coming through at around 59°F.

To pour, take a chalice-shaped glass such as those used to serve Trappist and other Belgian ales—though a large balloon wineglass will do just as well—and tilt it slightly. Pour the beer held from an inch or two above the glass's rim so that it flows smoothly, hitting a spot just off the center of the base of the glass.

Continue pouring as a single action, with as strong a flow and as few glugs as you can manage, until you start to see a slick of yeast advancing toward the neck of the bottle. Stop pouring.

With luck and practice this should leave you with a two-thirds-full glass of more or less clear beer sporting a sizable foaming "head," and half an inch of beer and sediment still in the bottle.

After enjoying all but the last mouthful of the beer, a true Belgian would swirl the sediment around in the bottle, add these cloudy dregs to the beer, and drink this in a single gulp. Personally, I prefer to pour the dregs down the sink.

HOW TO BE SURE IT'S A REAL TRAPPIST BEER

Trappist beers can be found at fine grocery stores such as Whole Foods. Just be sure to look for the small logo on the label that says AUTHENTIC TRAPPIST PRODUCT. Otherwise, it's easy to be misled by beer labels that feature monks and abbeys but aren't made by them. In fact, if there's a monk on the label, it isn't a Trappist beer—it's what is commonly called an abbey ale, an ale that is made by a commercial brewer in the style of a Trappist beer.

Commercial brewers like to put monks and abbeys on their labels because the true Trappist beers have such a high reputation for quality and taste. To confuse things even further, some monasteries that once made beer have licensed the names of their abbeys to commercial producers. So how does one find the real thing, and why does it matter?

Only seven beers in the world qualify as Authentic Trappist Products: Achel, Chimay, Orval, Rochefort, Westmalle, and Westvleteren, all in Belgium, and Koningshoeven in the Netherlands. Two other monastery food products use the logo: Orval cheese and liqueurs from Our Lady of Saint Joseph (aka Lilbosch Abbey) in the Netherlands.

The Authentic Trappist logo is more than just an advertising gimmick. It guarantees that a beer has been made at an abbey, either by monks and nuns or under their supervision, and that all profits are used to support Trappist monasteries (especially Trappist foundations in Africa) or for charity.

SUGGESTED ITINERARY: ABBEY BREW PUBS IN FLANDERS AND WALLONIA, BELGIUM

The best way to experience Belgian monastery beers is at an abbey brew pub. Monasteries that have brew pubs include Achel, Chimay, Orval, Westmalle, and Westvleteren. Another great way to taste monastery beers is as a guest on retreat, but be aware that not all monasteries accept both men and women for retreats.

There is no one perfect way to visit Belgian monasteries—you can drive to all the brew pubs, or take the train to one or two abbeys for a spiritual retreat, or concentrate on abbeys in only Dutch-speaking Belgium or only French-speaking Belgium—the possibilities are endless, and the beer is divine! Here are some suggested itineraries.

ITINERARY #1: FLANDERS (DUTCH-SPEAKING BELGIUM)

Flanders is easier to navigate than Wallonia for tourists who speak only English. It also has some magnificent monastery beers, including Westmalle Abbey's Dubbel and Tripel. Westmalle (www.trappistwestmalle.be) is a great place for travelers who want a silent spiritual retreat with plenty of opportunity for leisurely walks. It also has a marvelous brew pub, the Café Trappisten, for those who prefer to make this a day trip. Catch the local city bus in Antwerp and get off at the stop directly in front of the brew pub.

Achel (www.achelsekluis.org) is about an hour and a half from Westmalle by car (the nearest international train station is at Eindhoven in the Netherlands). It's a charming abbey that welcomes men and women for spiritual retreats. The brew pub is popular with locals, who often arrive on their bikes. It serves a wonderful beer that is available only on site, while the small grocery store next door sells the abbey's eponymous beer. Make sure to leave time for a stroll on the lovely heath that begins practically at the abbey's doorstep.

Westvleteren is the only abbey in Belgium where the monks still make the beer from start to finish. The abbey's beers—Trappist Westvleteren Blond, Trappist Westvleteren 8, and Trappist Westvleteren 12—are considered among the best in the world; however, they are not widely available. The best place to taste them is at the abbey brew pub. The monks also sell a limited quantity of bottled beer to the public, but only with advance reservations; for details, visit their website at www.sintsixtus.be. The abbey is not open to the public, but men who are interested in a religious retreat may contact the monks.

ITINERARY #2: WALLONIA (FRENCH-SPEAKING BELGIUM)

French-speaking Belgium is a wonderful place, but visitors who don't speak French may find some of the smaller towns difficult to navigate. Try taking the trains as much as possible if French is not an obstacle; for everyone else, driving may be the best way to reach these abbeys.

Orval (www.orval.be) is one of those places that is a must-see at least once in a lifetime. It is stunningly beautiful, makes one of the world's best beers, and welcomes both men and women for spiritual retreats. Toss in a great brew pub and you have a destination that is simply unforgettable. Contact the abbey in advance for information on hiring a taxi from the train station in Florenville.

Rochefort beer is made at Our Lady of Saint Rémy (www.trappistes-rochefort.com), a small jewel of an abbey whose beers taste like ambrosia—Rochefort 6, Rochefort 8, and the robust Rochefort 10, which should be drunk in moderation since it is more than 10 percent alcohol by volume! In one of the more curious monastic paradoxes, the abbey's gift shop doesn't carry Rochefort beer because the monks felt that doing so might disturb the contemplative atmosphere. Fortunately, Rochefort beers are becoming more widely available at fine grocery and liquor stores. The abbey has a charming guesthouse that is open to young men seeking a religious retreat; other visitors are welcome to attend services in one of Belgium's loveliest abbey churches.

Our Lady of Scourmont Abbey (www.chimay.com) makes Chimay beer. The abbey has a brew pub and a guesthouse that welcomes both men and women. Chimay makes three beers—Red, Triple, and the famous Blue, also known as Grande Réserve; the last, one of the world's great beers, is widely available at fine grocery stores. Chimay Red and Blue are excellent for cooking as well as drinking, while a glass of Chimay Triple makes a refreshing aperitif.

Braised Beef Cheeks with Sweet and Spicy Miso, Wildflower Honey-Glazed Carrots, and Toasted Sourdough Bread

Most people know that Charlie Trotter is one of the most innovative chefs in America and that his restaurant is one of the best reasons to visit Chicago. However, many people don't know that Chef Trotter once worked at a restaurant called The Monastery in Madison, Wisconsin. Whatever his inspiration, there's definitely something monastic about his commitment to helping others through the Charlie Trotter Culinary Education Foundation, which serves high school students and promotes culinary careers. He kindly shared this heavenly recipe.

BEEF CHEEKS

4 (12-ounce) beef cheeks (see Notes), trimmed of excess fat

Salt and freshly ground black pepper

About 4 tablespoons extra-virgin olive oil

2 medium carrots, chopped

2 celery ribs, chopped

1 medium onion, chopped

3 (11.2-ounce) bottles Chimay Blue beer (see Notes)

4 cups beef stock

SWEET AND SPICY MISO

¼ cup sugar

2½ tablespoons sherry vinegar

2 tablespoons orange juice

¼ cup diced Vidalia or other sweet onion

1 small Thai bird chile or other hot chile, seeded (optional) and finely chopped

¼ cup chunky white miso (see Notes)

GLAZED CARROTS

1 tablespoon unsalted butter

8 baby carrots or 4 small carrots

1 cup vegetable stock

¼ cup wildflower honey

Salt and freshly ground black pepper

4 thick slices sourdough bread

2 tablespoons extra-virgin olive oil

1. For the beef cheeks: Preheat the oven to 325°F.

2. Heat a 6-quart Dutch oven over medium-high heat until very hot. Pat the beef cheeks dry and season with salt and pepper. Add 2 tablespoons of the olive oil to the pot. Working in batches so as not to crowd the pot, sear the beef cheeks until well browned on all sides. Transfer the cheeks to a bowl as they are done. Add the remaining oil as needed to the pot for the second batch of beef.

3. Pour off most of the fat from the pot and add carrots, celery, and onions, scraping up the browned bits from the bottom of the pot. When you see the vegetables begin to lightly brown, deglaze with the beer. Reduce to 1 cup over high heat. Return the cheeks and any accumulated juices back into the pot. Add the beef stock and bring to a simmer. Cover the pot and braise in the oven until very tender, 2½ to 3 hours.

4. For the miso: While the beef is braising, put the sugar into a heavy medium pot and cook over medium heat, without disturbing, until the edges of the sugar in the pot begin to turn brown. Draw the sugar toward the center of the pot with

a heatproof spatula and stir until the sugar is completely melted and caramelized. Remove from the heat. Add the vinegar and orange juice to the pot very carefully, as the mixture will bubble up rapidly and steam and the caramel will seize into a hard piece. Add the onions and chiles, return pot to medium heat, and continue to cook, slowly stirring to dissolve the caramel back to liquid. Remove from the heat once the caramel is completely dissolved, add the miso to the pot, and stir until smooth. Transfer to a metal bowl and set over an ice bath to cool. Set aside.

5. For the carrots: Melt the butter in a small skillet (large enough to hold the carrots) over medium heat. Add the carrots and sweat them about 3 minutes. Add the stock and reduce the liquid by three-quarters. Stir in the honey to make a nice glaze. Season with salt and pepper and keep warm.

6. To finish and serve: Transfer the beef cheeks to a bowl, cover, and keep warm. Strain the braising liquid through a fine-mesh sieve into a bowl, pressing down on the solids with the back of a spoon. Return the liquid to the pot and reduce over high heat to 1 cup of sauce, about 20 minutes. Skim and discard any fat from the top of the sauce; keep warm.

7. Preheat the broiler. Brush the bread with the 2 tablespoons olive oil and arrange in a single layer on a sheet pan. Toast under the broiler until nicely browned. Set aside. On a separate pan, arrange the beef cheeks in a single layer and spread some miso on top of the cheeks (you may not need to use all of the miso; save any remainder, covered, in the refrigerator). Broil the beef until lightly browned, about 3 minutes. Arrange the beef cheeks with the glazed carrots on 4 plates, pour the sauce around cheeks, and serve with the toasted sourdough on the side.

Notes: Ask your butcher to order beef cheeks for you. Each trimmed cheek is about 12 ounces; however, if you are required to order a minimum weight untrimmed, keep in mind that each cheek may be up to 1 pound untrimmed.

State regulations for beer commerce vary, so monasteries rely on a network of local beer distributors. Look for Chimay beer in fine liquor and grocery stores such as Whole Foods, or ask them to order it for you.

Any quality chunky white miso found in the refrigerated section of a Japanese or Asian market will work well in this recipe. Charlie Trotter prefers to use three-year barley miso or chickpea miso from South River Miso. Visit www.southrivermiso.com to order special misos.

Roasted Cod Fillets, Smoked Trout Risotto, and Mussel Emulsion à la Trappiste

Ask people in the small town of Rochefort where the best place to eat is and they will all say Restaurant Couleur Basilic. From a seat in the lovely dining room, it quickly becomes clear that Chef Vincent Wauthy has found his vocation. This is food that is as beautiful and inventive as it is delicious. You can't buy beer at Rochefort Abbey—where the monks are especially fond of solitude—but you can attend a service in the lovely church and then dine here while raising a toast to the monks.

4 tablespoons unsalted butter, or to taste

½ cup Arborio rice

4 ounces skinless, boneless smoked trout (see Notes) or other mild smoked white
    fish, broken into bite-size pieces

4 (4-ounce) skinless, boneless cod fillets (about 1 inch thick)

1 tablespoon canola or vegetable oil

Salt and freshly ground black pepper

1 leek, white parts only, halved lengthwise, washed, and thinly sliced crosswise

1 (11.2-ounce) bottle Rochefort Trappiste 6 (see Notes) or other light Trappist
    beer

2 pounds cultivated mussels, scrubbed and bearded, discarding any mussels
    that have broken shells or remain open when tapped

2 tablespoons freshly grated Parmesan cheese

Parsley or chervil leaves for garnish

1. Preheat the oven to 450°F. Bring 3 cups of water to a boil in a small pot, then cover and keep warm over low heat.

2. Melt 1 tablespoon of the butter in a heavy medium pot over medium heat. Add the rice and cook, stirring to toast the rice, for 1 minute. Add the smoked trout and a ladleful, about 1 cup, of the hot water. Cook, stirring constantly, until the water is absorbed, then add another ladleful. Continue cooking and adding a ladleful of water at a time, stirring frequently, until the rice is tender and creamy-looking but still al dente, about 20 minutes. You may not need to use all of the water.

3. About 10 minutes into cooking the risotto, pat the cod dry and arrange in a single layer on a baking sheet. Drizzle with the oil and season generously with salt and pepper. Roast in the oven until cooked through, 8 to 10 minutes.

4. While the cod is roasting, melt 2 tablespoons of the remaining butter in a large skillet over medium heat, then add the leeks and sweat until crisp-tender, 2 to 3 minutes. Deglaze with ½ cup of the beer and let reduce for a minute or two, then add the mussels. Cover and cook, stirring occasionally, until the mussels open up wide, 3 to 5 minutes; transfer the mussels to a bowl as they are done. Discard any mussels that don't open. Add the remaining beer to the skillet and reduce until slightly thickened but still a tad brothy. Remove from the heat and whisk in the remaining tablespoon butter.

5. When the risotto is done, stir in the cheese and adjust the seasonings. Divide among 4 warmed plates. Put the cod on top of the risotto and spread the mussels and leeks around the fish. Pour the sauce over the cod and garnish with herbs. Serve immediately.

Notes: Smoked trout can be found in the seafood department of gourmet markets by the smoked salmon. To order online, visit www.brownetrading.com.

State regulations for beer commerce vary, so monasteries rely on a network of local beer distributors. Look for Rochefort beer in fine liquor and grocery stores such as Whole Foods, or ask them to order it for you. You can also visit www.merchantduvin.com to find a Rochefort distributor near you.

CARBONADES FLAMANDES
(Beef Stew from Flanders)

Michael Steele says Carbonades Flamandes is the signature beef stew from Flanders. Steele is manager of Markt, a Belgian hot spot in New York's Meatpacking District, where turn-of-the-century butcher shops share space with bars, restaurants, and some of New York's most fashionable residents. Markt serves this dish with another food that has made Belgium famous: hot, crispy fries. Belgians like to toss a few fries on their stew for good measure. Markt's recipe has been adapted here for home cooks.

1 pound sirloin steak, cut across the grain into strips

Salt and freshly ground black pepper

2 tablespoons all-purpose flour

4 tablespoons unsalted butter

1 medium Spanish onion, finely chopped

3 whole cloves garlic, crushed

¼ cup chopped fresh parsley, plus whole leaves for garnish

1 tablespoon chopped fresh thyme

1 (11.2-ounce bottle) Rochefort beer of your choice (see Note)
   or other Trappist beer (about 1½ cups)

2 tablespoons champagne vinegar or white wine vinegar

2 tablespoons Trappist red currant jelly or preserves

1. Season the steak generously with salt and pepper, then dredge in the flour, shaking off any excess. Melt 2 tablespoons of the butter in a large skillet over medium-high heat. Working in batches if necessary to avoid steaming the meat, sear the beef on both sides until golden brown, about a minute each side; transfer to a plate as they are done.

2. In the same skillet, melt the remaining 2 tablespoons butter over medium heat. Add the onion, season with salt and pepper, and toss to coat well. Partially cover the pan and cook the onions, stirring occasionally, until softened and golden brown, about 25 minutes.

3. Return the beef and any juices that may have collected back to the skillet of onions. Stir in the garlic, chopped parsley, thyme, and beer. Cook over medium heat, stirring occasionally, until the sauce has thickened, about 20 minutes.

4. Stir in the vinegar and preserves and cook for another minute. Adjust the seasonings. Discard the garlic, garnish the dish with the parsley leaves, and serve immediately with french fries, if you wish.

Note: State regulations for beer commerce vary, so monasteries rely on a network of local beer distributors. Look for Rochefort beer in fine liquor and grocery stores such as Whole Foods, or ask them to order it for you. You can also visit www.merchantduvin.com to find a Rochefort distributor near you.

Ask Belgians which Trappist beer is their favorite and many will say Chimay. However, some beer experts say Chimay's quality has slipped as production has increased and fault Chimay for being too commercial (the brewery's secular marketing team ran a TV ad, which is unthinkable in most Trappist circles). Nevertheless, the abbot runs a tight ship and the monastery's beers are very good. This is a fun Belgian twist on Irish whiskey. For more Chimay recipes, visit www.chimay.com.

1¼ cups Chimay Blue (see Note)
1 tablespoon brown sugar
Pinch of ground cinnamon
1 cup strong coffee
Heavy cream

Heat the beer in a small pot over medium-high heat until hot but not boiling. Add the brown sugar and a pinch of cinnamon. Pour the mixture into a large cup of hot strong coffee. Carefully top with some cream.

Note: State regulations for beer commerce vary, so monasteries rely on a network of local beer distributors. Look for Chimay beer in fine liquor and grocery stores such as Whole Foods, or ask them to order it for you.

Chef Ralf Kuettel has made his mark at Trestle on Tenth in Manhattan, where he likes to cook with fine Belgian beers. His recipe for veal kidneys uses just enough Trappist ale to give the dish its distinct flavor. This recipe is quick to prepare and makes great comfort food on a cold winter's eve; diners at Kuettel's restaurant can be seen sopping up every last drop of the dish with crusty pieces of bread. Serve it with the remaining Trappist ale.

1 pound cleaned veal kidney (see Notes), sliced lengthwise and
    white membranes removed (about 1½ cups)

Salt and freshly ground white pepper

1 tablespoon canola oil

1 tablespoon diced shallots

¼ cup Chimay beer of your choice (see Notes) or other Trappist ale

1 tablespoon veal stock (see Notes)

2 tablespoons heavy cream

1 teaspoon unsalted butter

Crusty bread or roasted potatoes (optional)

1. Pat the kidney slices dry. Generously season the kidneys with salt and pepper. Heat a medium pan over medium-high heat, add the oil and kidneys to the hot pan, and sear evenly. Add the shallots and deglaze with the beer. Stir in the veal stock and heavy cream and simmer for 2 minutes. Remove the pan from the heat and whisk in the butter. Adjust the seasonings and serve immediately with good crusty bread or roasted potatoes, if you like.

Notes: Ask your butcher to set aside or special-order veal kidneys.

State regulations for beer commerce vary, so monasteries rely on a network of local beer distributors. Look for Chimay beer in fine liquor and grocery stores such as Whole Foods, or ask them to order it for you.

Veal stock can be made from the base Glace de Veau Gold or Glace de Viande Gold, by More than Gourmet (www.morethangourmet.com). It can also be found in the broth/stock section of gourmet markets.

SAINT BENEDICT ABBEY, AKA ACHEL HERMITAGE

NEAR ACHEL, BELGIUM, AND EINDHOVEN, THE NETHERLANDS

The monks who built this brewery knew exactly what they wanted—stainless steel tanks, high-quality hops, mills to grind the malt—but they overlooked one thing: The Netherlands is just across the border, and that means hundreds of thousands of thirsty Dutch and at least as many bicycles are only a stone's throw away. The monks soon became worried that the combination of beer and bikes might not be such a good idea along the busy Dutch–Belgian border (which runs right through the abbey). Happily, the answer has not been to stop serving beer but rather to serve a light beer on tap, and it's pumped directly into the café from the brewery. It's worth coming here just to taste beer this fresh, and sharing the experience with a crowd of mildly tipsy bikers is half the fun.

Hermits lived here long before the first bikers arrived; this secluded spot in the Limburg province of Flanders was home to a community of hermits from 1686 until the French Revolution. There's a lovely little bronze statue in front of the guesthouse that depicts the Trappists who arrived on foot in 1846 from Westmalle Abbey and founded Saint Benedict Abbey on the site of the old Achel Hermitage; the monks lean on their walking sticks and their weariness is palpable, but so is their resolve. Most of the land that the monks once farmed is now a nature preserve where guests on retreat can walk, bike, jog, or simply sit and watch the remarkably flat but beautiful landscape of heath and woods. The brewery was founded in 1998, and is thus the youngest of the Belgian Trappist breweries, but Achel is quickly gaining an international reputation for its beers.

Achel's brewery is high-tech but fits into a space that is not much larger than a two-car garage. Everyone should come to the brewery's pub once in a lifetime to share the blond or brown beers on tap with friends; the blond ale is especially refreshing and at 5 percent alcohol isn't likely to knock one off one's bike. Achel is most famous for its stronger blond beer in a bottle, which is nicely hopped and slightly cloudy (this beer is unfiltered, so any cloudiness simply adds to its character). The monks fill large bottles of Achel beer at the monastery, but smaller bottles are filled off-site at a nearby brewery; nevertheless, the beer is brewed entirely within the monastic enclosure and qualifies for the Authentic Trappist Product label, and even better, the master brewer here is still a monk.

If there is any place where one can chat with God while seated on a bicycle, this is it. The abbey has bikes that guests can use, and while one might worry that a bike could introduce guests on retreat to the possibility of haste or even competition (neither of which are very monastic qualities), the abbey's well-worn bikes force guests to a contemplative pace no matter how hard they pedal. Nevertheless, walking remains the most contemplative form of transportation, and it's a pleasure to hike through the lowland heath, whose winter palette of rich browns and golds calls Rembrandt to mind.

For anyone who has ever had a really bad corporate job, it's hard to understand why more young men don't come to Achel to stay for good and work in the brewery. Imagine going to work and participating in God's creation every day by brewing a world-class beer, using only the best ingredients without artificial flavors or chemicals, and making people's lives happier with the final product. Now imagine doing all of that and also getting to pray in a lovely winter chapel that is one of the most intimate of any abbey and where one never tires of seeing the delicate Gothic arches overhead or hearing the psalms sung under the soaring brick arches of the grand church that is used in summer.

It may take an act of grace to lead a few good-hearted men to Achel in these modern times. If they come, they will discover that there is nothing to fear in Saint Benedict's rule. Saint Benedict himself says his rule is intended to establish a "school for the Lord's service," and adds, "We hope to set down nothing harsh, nothing burdensome. The good of all concerned, however, may prompt us to a little strictness in order to amend faults and to safeguard love. Do not be daunted immediately by fear and run away from the road that leads to salvation." One way to think of the rule is simply as an invitation—to a way of life that is different from that of the world's, to a way of work that is a form of prayer, and to a communal life that is based on love. Who wouldn't raise a toast to that?

FOOD PRODUCTS: Beer

GUESTHOUSE: Yes, M/F

WEBSITE: www.achelsekluis.org

ORDER: Visit www.sheltonbrothers.com for a distributor near you.

E-MAIL: info@sheltonbrothers.com

GUESTHOUSE E-MAIL: gastenhuis@achelsekluis.org

NOTE: For international calls, first dial 011 from the United States or 00 from Europe, then 32 for Belgium, followed by the local phone number listed below; if the local number begins with a zero, drop it when dialing from abroad.

GUESTHOUSE PHONE: 11 800 766

St. Benedict Abbey/Achel Hermitage

De Kluis 1

3930 Hamont-Achel

Belgium

M. F. K. Fisher once wrote that she could almost live on soup alone. For those of us who could almost live on beer alone, what could be better than combining the two? Brother Victor-Antoine d'Avila-Latourrette of Our Lady of the Resurrection Monastery in upstate New York kindly shared this recipe. It is adapted from his book Twelve Months of Monastery Soups.

1 (750-ml) bottle Achel Extra (about 3½ cups; see Note) or your favorite Achel or
    Rochefort beer

2 tablespoons sugar

4 large egg yolks

6 tablespoons crème fraîche or heavy cream

½ teaspoon ground cinnamon

½ teaspoon salt

Freshly ground black pepper

1. Pour the beer, 2 cups water, and the sugar into a large soup pot and bring to a boil over medium-high heat, stirring to dissolve the sugar. Remove from the heat.

2. Beat the yolks, crème fraîche, cinnamon, and salt in a bowl. Slowly add ½ cup of the hot beer mixture to the egg mixture, whisking until well combined.

3. Pour the egg mixture into the pot of beer, stirring constantly, and cook for a couple more minutes over low heat without bringing it to a boil. Season with salt and pepper to taste. Serve immediately.

Note: State regulations for beer commerce vary, so monasteries rely on a network of local beer distributors. Look for Achel beer in fine liquor and grocery stores such as Whole Foods, or ask them to order it for you. You can also visit www.sheltonbrothers.com to find an Achel distributor near you.

Saint Lioba Beer and Mushroom Soup   *Serves 4 to 6*

For a soup that feeds the stomach and the soul, this one is hard to beat. It's delicious, hearty, and healthy, another recipe from Brother Victor-Antoine d'Avila-Latourrette's Twelve Months of Monastery Soups.

    10 ounces button mushrooms, cleaned and chopped
    1 large onion, finely chopped
    6 tablespoons olive oil
    1 (750-ml) bottle Achel Extra (about 3½ cups; see Note) or your favorite Achel or
        Rochefort beer
    2½ cups vegetable stock
    1 bay leaf
    2 large eggs
    ½ cup heavy cream
    ¼ cup chopped fresh parsley
    Salt and freshly ground black pepper
    ½ cup grated Gruyère cheese for garnish

1. Sweat the mushrooms and onions in the olive oil in a soup pot over medium heat until the onions are soft. Add the beer, stock, and bay leaf and increase the heat to high. Bring the soup to a boil, then reduce the heat and simmer slowly for about 20 minutes.

2. Meanwhile, beat the eggs with the cream in a bowl. Slowly add ½ cup of the hot soup to the egg mixture and blend thoroughly.

3. Pour the mixture into the pot of soup, mixing well. Add the chopped parsley, season with salt and pepper to taste, and mix well. Continue stirring for a few minutes.

4. Remove the bay leaf and serve the soup hot with some grated cheese sprinkled on top of each serving.

Note: State regulations for beer commerce vary, so monasteries rely on a network of local beer distributors. Look for Achel beer in fine liquor and grocery stores such as Whole Foods, or ask them to order it for you. You can also visit www.sheltonbrothers.com to find an Achel distributor near you.

ORVAL ABBEY

NEAR FLORENVILLE, BELGIUM

This is a monastery fit for angels. A guest can't help imagining that the angels wait until all the mortals have gone to bed, and then come down to frolic in a place where one feels several steps closer to heaven. Some of them probably stroll among the ruins of the medieval abbey and marvel at the rose window whose scalloped edges now frame nothing but open sky, while others may prefer to sit by the waters of Orval's famous spring and retell the legend that gives the abbey its name. Or perhaps they are fond of the abbey's serene reflecting pool and Japanese dry rock garden. All of these are also good reasons for mortals to visit; however, even angels would agree that the best reason to come is one that is earthly but tastes like heaven: Orval beer.

Orval Abbey was founded in 1070 by monks who originally came from Italy. It now belongs to the Order of Cistercians of the Strict Observance (Trappists). The medieval abbey was destroyed during the French Revolution, but monks reclaimed the spot in 1926; they added a brewery in 1931 as a way to fund the construction of their new abbey. Orval beer is brewed and bottled entirely within the monastery and qualifies for the Authentic Trappist Product label, but the brewery has always employed locals and is a major source of jobs in this remote corner of Wallonia. One of the monks helps manage the brewery, where he fields calls on his cell phone and troubleshoots just like any other business executive—except this one is wearing a monk's habit.

Like Leonardo da Vinci's greatest works of art, Orval is part science, part art, and wholly sublime. The architect, Henry Vaes, designed the monastery in a classic Cistercian style. Vaes looked to some of the greatest examples of Cistercian architecture for inspiration, including Fontenay Abbey for Orval's church, the ruins of Villers-la-Ville for the brewery, and the Cistercian barn of Ter Doest (between Bruges and the North Sea) for the abbey's large barn.

That helps explain the stunning beauty of the place, but nothing quite prepares one for the unusual Madonna who graces the church façade: she stands two stories high and is carved from golden sandstone, like an Egyptian queen. Just as beautiful is the large triangular reflecting pool that lies between the church and guesthouse. It's as though the architect had composed a symphony out of stone, and the reflecting pool is the perfect note that holds it all together. Another lovely feature here is the long covered walkway that connects the retreat house to the church and keeps guests dry even when it rains.

Orval is especially beautiful after evening prayers when Grand Silence settles over the monastery and not a whisper disturbs the calm surface of the reflecting pool. This time of night might as well be called the angel's hour. The stars shine like jewels in a mantle fit for the Queen of Heaven, and the place is simply humbling in its perfection.

This is as good a time as any for a guest on retreat to contemplate one's blessings as well as one's sins. Hopefully the former outweigh the latter, but if not you're in luck—the monastery's world-class beer can take the edge off of one's woes and guests on retreat drink it at meals (except on fast days).

Orval brews only one beer, and it starts with water from the Matilda Fountain, a natural spring that flows on the abbey grounds. The spring gets its name from Matilda of Tuscany, who did her own version of a spiritual retreat here in the eleventh century. That's when she accidentally dropped her wedding ring into the spring, where legend says a trout magically retrieved it in response to her fervent prayers. Guests who reach Orval by train can grab a beer at the train station café in Libramont and take home a souvenir beer coaster with the famous Orval trout on it; this is also a fun way to pass the time for anyone who happens to miss the connecting train to Florenville, which runs only once every two hours (just be aware that small-town cafés in Belgium may be filled with cigarette smoke).

The first thing one notices about Orval beer is its delightfully refreshing aroma. No matter how weary a visitor may be from jet lag or the stress of modern life, this beer is a sure pick-me-up. It is made with water, malted barley, hops, sugar, and yeast, and at just 6.2 percent alcohol it's light enough to consider having a second bottle. The lovely aroma and lively bitter taste come from a method called dry hopping, whereby large sacks of high-quality hop flowers are added during the second fermentation and steeped in the beer much as one would brew a pot of herbal tea. It is during this phase that a wild yeast called *Brettanomyces* is also added, which gives the beer a funky quality; this is a slow-acting yeast, which means that the flavor of Orval changes as it matures.

Orval is stored at the brewery for three to four weeks before being sold and undergoes a third fermentation in the bottle. This resting period alone sets Orval apart from the "wet air" beers of titanic commercial breweries such as InBev (for a very funny and biting account of InBev's business tactics, read Tim Webb's *Good Beer Guide: Belgium*). The more time one spends at monasteries the more one learns to think like a monk, and monks would never sell a beer before its time. In fact, locals who are in the know show up at the Orval brewery to buy bottles that have been aged six months, when the monks say the beer really hits its stride.

The brewery is open to the public for tours only twice a year; however, there is a pub down the street where day-trippers can swap stories about their favorite Trappist beers. Of course, there's nothing quite like doing a spiritual retreat at Orval: this monastery is an oasis of peace even when late winter rains lend the place an appropriately Lenten mood. The liturgy at this time of year says "God, grant us a simple heart so that we may not serve the idols of our times." This sounds easy enough, but in practice human nature is anything but simple-hearted. It takes hard work to resist the marketing messages that distract good-hearted people from what they might otherwise seek: to love one another.

Monks and nuns provide a witness to God here on earth and they experience God as members of a community; even Saint Bruno took six companions with him into the French Alps to live as a community of hermits when he founded the Carthusian order. If it is possible to experience God through communal life—and the monks here are living proof—then it's a mystery why more men don't come to Orval to stay for good. Without monks at its helm, the abbey's brewery would become like any other company where managers seek only to maximize profits. Perhaps some young man who comes here hoping to taste one of the world's great beers may have an epiphany of a different kind. The angels are surely keeping watch for him.

FOOD PRODUCTS: Beer

GUESTHOUSE: Yes, M/F

WEBSITE: www.orval.be

ORDER: Orval is available at fine liquor and grocery stores such as Whole Foods, or visit www.merchantduvin.com to find a distributor near you.

GUESTHOUSE E-MAIL: hotellerie@orval.be

NOTE: For international calls, first dial 011 from the United States or 00 from Europe, then 32 for Belgium, followed by the local phone number listed below; if the local number begins with a zero, drop it when dialing from abroad.

GUESTHOUSE PHONE: 61 32 51 10

Orval Abbey

B-6823 Villers-devant-Orval

Belgium

Orval beer is so delicious that one may find it difficult to spare any for cooking. Try not to overindulge, and use whatever you manage not to drink in this lovely recipe. It has been adapted from a delightful cookbook, Flavors from Orval *by Nicole Darchambeau, available in the abbey gift shop and at www.heavengourmet.com.*

1 large apple, preferably Jonagold
2½ tablespoons unsalted butter
4 chicken livers, washed and patted dry
Salt and freshly ground black pepper
⅓ cup Orval beer (see Note)
Toasted bread (optional)

1. Peel the apple, cut into quarters, remove the core, and cut each wedge into 3 wedges.

2. Melt 1 tablespoon of the butter in a small skillet over medium-high heat and add the apples. Toss to coat with butter and cook until lightly browned, about 8 minutes. Transfer the apples to a plate, cover to keep warm, and set aside.

3. Generously season the livers with salt and pepper. Melt 1 tablespoon of the remaining butter in the skillet over medium-high heat, add the livers, and sear until golden and just springy to the touch (but still faintly rosy on the inside). Transfer to a plate and cover to keep warm. Deglaze the pan with the beer and reduce, scraping the browned bits from the bottom of the pan, until the liquid is just glazing the pan. Remove from the heat and whisk in the remaining ½ tablespoon butter.

4. Arrange the apple slices in the center of 2 plates and top with the chicken livers. Spoon the sauce over the livers. Serve with lightly toasted bread, if you like.

Note: State regulations for beer commerce vary, so monasteries rely on a network of local beer distributors. Look for Orval beer in fine liquor and grocery stores, or ask them to order it for you. You can also visit www.merchantduvin.com to find an Orval distributor near you.

ABBEY OF OUR BELOVED LADY OF THE SACRED HEART, AKA WESTMALLE

NEAR ANTWERP, BELGIUM

If one is going to make only one pilgrimage in a lifetime, this is the place to do it. The monastery has its own brewery pub, the Café Trappisten, that serves pilgrims with food and beer just as abbeys did in the Middle Ages. Of course, modern pilgrims have several advantages over their predecessors: the beer is better now, thanks to the monastery's renowned ales; the food is delicious, and it's as easy to get here as it is to board a public bus in Antwerp. This makes coming to Westmalle not quite as challenging as, say, going out into the desert to find God, but it's a good place to come in from the spiritual desert of modern life. Pilgrims often traveled by foot, and walking down the lovely tree-lined lane that leads to the abbey gate is still the best way to arrive, so pack light and take the public bus.

The Trappist Abbey of Westmalle was founded in 1794 and belongs to the Order of Cistercians of the Strict Observance (Trappists). This part of Belgium is called Flanders and the locals here speak a colloquial form of Dutch. The liturgy is also in Dutch and

the monks speak little or no English, but one can follow along with their prayers in spirit if not in letter; in fact, it's so pleasant to listen to the monks sing the Daily Office that a recent visitor was temporarily seized with a desire to study the language (until recalling that the only phrase she had learned to pronounce correctly in Dutch was "Good morning"). Brewing began here in 1860 and the abbey is credited with having invented the blond Tripel, a style of Belgian ale that is pale in color, strong in alcohol, and fairly bitter; whether or not Westmalle actually invented the Tripel, it has since perfected it.

Their refreshingly bitter Tripel packs a wallop at 9.5 percent alcohol and is made with high-quality real hops (flowers, not extract or pellets) that come from the Czech Republic and eastern Germany. The brewery staff works hard to make this beer as aesthetically pleasing as it is thirst-quenching, so remember to serve it at cellar temperature (in a Westmalle glass if possible) and never put it in the fridge, where the beer will become cloudy. Westmalle also makes an eye-catching dark ale called a Dubbel, whose bitter notes are more flirtatious than aggressive; the Tripel and Dubbel

are brewed and bottled entirely within the monastery and meet the requirements for the Authentic Trappist Product label. A third beer, the Extra, is not for sale but is served to guests on retreat; it's a rich coppery gold color, has a lovely aroma, and pairs well with the simple but hearty food.

Everyone who works here has a favorite story about how the monks do business. An oft-cited example is the way the monks (who no longer work in the brewery but serve on its board of directors) decided to cap production despite increased demand, a decision that would be unheard of in the commercial world. Then there was the time the marketing staff wanted to sell the Tripel in Champagne-size bottles and label it "Réserve," like a fine wine; the monks said yes to the larger bottle but no to the luxury label (interestingly, the beer ages somewhat differently in larger bottles than small ones, so sample both). Westmalle's monks are also renowned for their charity and have sponsored everything from major medical research to an event that allows blind people to experience tandem cycling with a seeing partner.

Westmalle is the only Trappist monastery in Belgium where the monks still make cheese. This seems an obvious choice when one sees that the abbey is surrounded by lush green pastures that are remarkably flat and look like a cow's version of the Elysian fields. The monks use solely unpasteurized raw milk from their own herd of about one hundred cows, which are a breed called Groningse Blaarkoppen (Dutch, of course); at least one monk is rumored to know every cow by name. The cheese is sold exclusively at the Café Trappisten and in a small store inside the abbey entrance, but guests on retreat get to enjoy it with their meals. The cheese subtly changes color and flavor depending on the season and whether the cows are eating grass or hay, and it is worth tasting at different times of year. It can be bought mild or aged.

A Latin inscription above the monastery's entrance quotes the gospel of Luke: "Unless you repent, you will all perish." At first this seems a rather forbidding message for a place where everyone and everything strikes one as being exceedingly gentle. However, it begins to makes more sense as one spends time here reading, contemplating, and listening to the Psalms. Perhaps monks are able to act gently, speak gently, and live gently—or as Buddhist monk Thich Nhat Hanh says, even tread the earth gently—precisely because they have repented. The act of repentance requires admitting one's faults but also accepting one's graces, and it comes more easily to those who have a sense of awe about the world and are humble. From a monk's point of view, Luke's message is one of hope and joy as well as repentance.

Even in a dense fog, this abbey is beautiful. It is made of brick, as are other Belgian abbeys that were built in areas that lacked good stone quarries. One can follow the brick walls around the abbey, walking in a large square pattern that is simple yet surprisingly contemplative, or take longer walks along the small paved roads that also serve bikers, joggers, and locals who come here to walk their dogs and gather acorns. Sometimes the fog grows so thick that the church disappears entirely, but a guest can still follow its bell like a spiritual foghorn. As one turns back toward church for Vespers, one is reminded of a saying that recounts how Saint Benedict loved valleys while Saint Bernard loved mountains. While there are no mountains here, the earth is flat in a way that reminds one that sometimes the mountain is a spiritual one.

FOOD PRODUCTS: Beer

GUESTHOUSE: Yes, M/F

WEBSITE: www.trappistwestmalle.be

ORDER: Westmalle is available at fine grocery stores such as Whole Foods, or visit www.merchantduvin.com for a distributor near you.

E-MAIL: info@trappistwestmalle.be (for general inquiries)

NOTE: For international calls, first dial 011 from the United States or 00 from Europe, then 32 for Belgium, followed by the local phone number listed below; if the local number begins with a zero, drop it when dialing from abroad.

PHONE: (0)3 312 92 00 (for general inquiries)

GUESTHOUSE PHONE: (0)3 312 92 09

Westmalle Abbey

Antwerpsesteenweg 496

B-2390 Westmalle

Belgium

According to beer expert and author Jef van den Steen, Westmalle's Tripel is a complex beer with competing flavors: the fruity aroma of ripe banana, the delicate bitterness of hops, and the sweetness of malt. He says the Tripel's creamy, mellow character is balanced by a fruity, acidic touch reminiscent of orange and that a beer like this one calls for a bold, daring dessert! This recipe has been adapted from Westmalle Trappist: Met Eenvoudige en Lekkere Eenpansgerechten *(Delicious One-Dish Meals Made Easy) by Stefaan Couttenye and Jef van den Steen.*

1 cup sugar

½ cup plus 2 tablespoons dark rum

½ cup plus 2 tablespoons Westmalle Tripel (see Note)

Zest of half a lemon, peeled in wide strips with a vegetable peeler

Zest of half an orange, peeled in wide strips with a vegetable peeler

4 ripe but still firm bananas

4 small slices of fruitcake

4 scoops chocolate ice cream

Toasted sliced almonds for garnish (optional)

1. Combine the sugar, rum, beer, and zests in a large nonstick skillet. Cook over medium-high heat, stirring occasionally, until a thick syrup forms, about 15 minutes.

2. Remove the zests and add the peeled bananas. Cook, spooning the sauce over the bananas often and shaking pan to gently roll the bananas for a few minutes, until they are well glazed. Carefully remove the bananas from the skillet and arrange on 4 plates. Remove the skillet from the heat.

3. Briefly dip both sides of the cake slices in the syrup so it soaks up a little bit. Place the cake on the plates with the bananas. Drizzle the remaining syrup on top.

4. Serve with a scoop of chocolate ice cream and sprinkle with toasted sliced almonds, if using. This dessert can be served hot or cold.

Note: State regulations for beer commerce vary, so monasteries rely on a network of local beer distributors. Look for Westmalle beer in fine liquor and grocery stores, or ask them to order it for you. You can also visit www.merchantduvin.com to find a distributor near you.

Americans call this dish French toast, the French say pain perdu *(lost bread), and the Dutch say it is bread that has been "earned." Whatever one chooses to call it, this is a delicious way to salvage old bread. Make this with a good raisin bread like* cramique *(a Flemish version of brioche) and replace some of the milk with Trappist beer for a sophisticated twist on a favorite classic. This recipe has been adapted from* Westmalle Trappist: Met Eenvoudige en Lekkere Eenpansgerechten *(Delicious One-Dish Meals Made Easy) by Stefaan Couttenye and Jef van den Steen.*

CRÈME ANGLAISE

⅓ cup milk

½ cup heavy cream

1-inch piece vanilla bean, split, beans scraped, seeds and bean reserved

2 large egg yolks

1½ tablespoon granulated sugar

FRENCH TOAST

⅔ cup Westmalle Dubbel (see Note)

⅔ cup milk

4 egg yolks

4 tablespoons granulated sugar

Pinch of ground cinnamon

4 thick slices of stale brioche with raisins or other thick-sliced raisin bread

About 1 tablespoon unsalted butter, melted

½ cup brown sugar

Mocha ice cream (optional)

1. For the crème anglaise: Combine the milk and cream in a small heavy saucepan. Add the vanilla bean and scraped seeds and bring to a simmer. Remove from the heat.

2. Whisk the yolks and sugar well in a medium bowl. Gradually whisk ½ cup of the hot milk mixture into the yolk mixture, then return to the saucepan, whisking constantly. Stir over low heat until the mixture thickens and leaves a path on the back of a spoon when a finger is pulled across the spoon, about 5 minutes. Do not let the mixture boil or the eggs will cook. Strain into a bowl, discarding the vanilla bean, and chill, covered.

3. For the French toast: Beat the beer, milk, egg yolks, sugar, and cinnamon in a large bowl until smooth and creamy. Briefly soak the brioche in this batter (soak a little longer if it is very stale). Remove and let excess batter drip off.

4. Heat a large skillet or griddle over medium heat until hot but not smoking. Brush the skillet or griddle with some of the melted butter, then put as many pieces of the soaked bread as fit into the pan or griddle without crowding. Generously sprinkle the tops with brown sugar (about 1 tablespoon per side of bread). Flip and sprinkle the other side with brown sugar. Continue to turn the bread every 3 to 5 minutes, brushing the skillet or griddle with butter as necessary, until both sides are well caramelized. Be sure to use moderate heat, otherwise the *pain perdu* will burn and it will be lost for good!

5. Serve on a pool of crème anglaise with a scoop of mocha ice cream, if desired.

Note: State regulations for beer commerce vary, so monasteries rely on a network of local beer distributors. Look for Westmalle beer in fine liquor and grocery stores, or ask them to order it for you. You can also visit www.merchantduvin.com to find a Westmalle distributor near you.

Monks and nuns who follow the Rule of Saint Benedict are vegetarians because Saint Benedict says that only monks who are ill should eat meat. American monk Thomas Merton wrote that a single sardine once showed up on his plate when he was in the monastic infirmary; he wasn't sure if it was his ration of meat or a mistake. This recipe is a reason to celebrate being vegetarian rather than to regret it. It has been adapted from Westmalle Trappist: Met Eenvoudige en Lekkere Eenpansgerechten (Delicious One-Dish Meals Made Easy) by Stefaan Couttenye and Jef van den Steen.

1 small red pepper

1 small yellow pepper

1½ cups short- or medium-grain rice

4 tablespoons extra-virgin olive oil

Salt

1 to 2 tablespoons ground cumin, to taste

1 to 2 tablespoons paprika, to taste

5 cloves garlic, finely chopped

⅔ cup vegetable broth, heated

¼ cup plus 2 tablespoons Westmalle Tripel (see Note)

A few threads of saffron, lightly crushed

1 carrot, sliced into ¼-inch coins

1 zucchini, sliced into ¼-inch coins

1 cup frozen green peas, thawed

¾ cup fresh or frozen corn kernels, thawed if frozen

12 black olives

8 oil-packed sun-dried tomatoes, drained and chopped

Freshly ground black pepper

½ cup chopped fresh parsley

1. Preheat the broiler. Put the peppers in a small baking pan and put under the broiler, turning them over occasionally, until blistered and a little charred on all sides. Remove from the oven, transfer to a bowl, and cover. When cool enough to handle, peel the peppers, discarding the skins, stems, and seeds, then cut into long strips. Set aside.

2. While the peppers are broiling, combine the rice, 2½ cups cold water, 1 tablespoon of the olive oil, and a couple of pinches of salt in a medium saucepan. Bring to a boil, then reduce the heat and simmer, uncovered, stirring often. When all the water has been absorbed, about 15 minutes, the rice should be done.

3. Meanwhile, heat the remaining 3 tablespoons olive oil in a 12-inch skillet. Add the cumin and paprika and cook for two to three minutes. Add the garlic and stir to coat. Cook for 1 minute, then gradually add half the hot broth, the beer, and saffron, stirring continuously. The spices will form a thin paste. Add the carrots, stirring to coat, and cook for 3 to 4 minutes. Then add the zucchini and cook for 2 minutes. Stir in the green peas and corn and cook until the vegetables are just cooked.

4. Add the rice to the vegetables and mix. If the rice starts to dry out, add more of the vegetable broth. Add the olives and sun-dried tomatoes and season with salt and pepper. Arrange the roasted peppers on top and sprinkle with the parsley. Serve in the skillet.

Note: State regulations for beer commerce vary, so monasteries rely on a network of local beer distributors. Look for Westmalle beer in fine liquor and grocery stores, or ask them to order it for you. You can also visit www.merchantduvin.com to find a Westmalle distributor near you.

This recipe takes a hearty Belgian salad from Liège and adds a hint of beer. It can be served as a main course or it can accompany a meat dish. Either way, it tastes divine! This recipe is another one adapted from Westmalle Trappist: Met Eenvoudige en Lekkere Eenpansgerechten *(Delicious One-Dish Meals Made Easy) by Stefaan Couttenye and Jef van den Steen.*

Salt

1½ pounds green beans or haricots verts, trimmed

1½ pounds small new potatoes, scrubbed

3 tablespoons unsalted butter

1 onion, thinly sliced

Freshly ground black pepper

A few sprigs of summer savory

12 ounces thick-sliced bacon, cut crosswise into ¼-inch-thick strips

2/3 cup Westmalle Tripel (see Note)

3 tablespoons white wine vinegar

1. Bring a large pot of salted water to a boil, then blanch the green beans until crisp-tender, 3 to 4 minutes. Shock the green beans in a large bowl of ice water, then drain well.

2. Pour out the water and put the potatoes into the pot. Cover with cold water, add salt, then bring to a simmer. Cook until the potatoes are slightly underdone and the tip of a knife hits a slight resistance when pierced into the center of a potato, 8 to 10 minutes. Drain well. When cool enough to handle, peel the potatoes if you like and then slice into ¼-inch-thick rounds. Set aside.

3. Preheat the oven to 450°F. Melt 2 tablespoons of the butter in a 12-inch skillet, add the onion, season with salt and pepper, and cook until softened, about 10 minutes. Add the green beans, toss to mix well, and transfer to a 9 × 13-inch baking dish.

4. Melt the remaining tablespoon butter in the same skillet, brown the potatoes, and season with salt and pepper, and a few sprigs of savory. Mix with the green beans and onions.

5. Cook the bacon in the same skillet until browned and transfer with a slotted spoon to the baking dish. Discard the bacon grease or save for another use. Deglaze the skillet with the beer and vinegar, scraping up the browned bits on the bottom of the pan, and reduce until the liquid just glazes the pan. Pour over the salad and mix well. Heat the dish in the oven for a few minutes and serve very hot. Garnish with the remaining sprigs of savory.

Note: State regulations for beer commerce vary, so monasteries rely on a network of local beer distributors. Look for Westmalle beer in fine liquor and grocery stores, or ask them to order it for you. You can also visit www.merchantduvin.com to find a Westmalle distributor near you.

Wrapping the salmon en papillote (in a sheet of aluminum foil or parchment paper) helps the flavors of orange zest and hops permeate its flesh, giving the salmon an exotic touch. Make sure to fold the papillote so that it is watertight. Foil is easy to seal tightly and therefore preferable to parchment paper. This recipe has been adapted from West-malle Trappist: Met Eenvoudige en Lekkere Eenpansgerechten (Delicious One-Dish Meals Made Easy) by Stefaan Couttenye and Jef van den Steen.

Zest of ⅓ of an orange, peeled in wide strips with a vegetable peeler

½ tablespoon unsalted butter

1 (11.2-ounce) bottle Westmalle Tripel (about 1⅓ cups; see Note)

⅓ cup fish stock

4 (6-ounce) center-cut boneless, skinless salmon fillets

Salt and freshly ground black pepper

2 scallions

1 tomato, seeded and diced

4 ounces small button mushrooms, wiped clean, stemmed, and quartered

2 tablespoons chopped fresh cilantro

Canola or vegetable oil

Hollandaise sauce or small boiled potatoes (optional)

1. Bring a small pot of water to a boil. Quickly blanch the zest in boiling water, then shock under cold running water. Repeat this process three times, starting with fresh cold water each time. Drain the zest, pat dry, and slice into very thin long strips.

2. Preheat the oven to 450°F. Spread out 4 pieces of heavy-duty aluminum foil,

each about 12 inches long. Generously grease the center of each piece of foil with butter. Combine the beer and stock in a container with a pouring spout and set aside.

3. Halve the salmon fillets horizontally so you have 2 flat pieces. Generously season both sides of each piece of salmon with salt and pepper. Place the bottom halves on the buttered sides of the foil. If the salmon bottom is longer than the top half, fold the thinner flap of the bottom half of salmon over itself so the two pieces are roughly the same length. Sprinkle the salmon with some scallions, tomatoes, a few quartered mushrooms, the julienned orange zest, and chopped fresh cilantro. Season again with salt and pepper and then cover with the top half of the fillets.

4. Fold up the aluminum foil tightly, leaving an opening at the top just large enough to pour in the beer-stock mixture. Place each parcel in a single layer in a lightly greased heavy ovenproof 12-inch skillet or small roasting pan (preferably not nonstick). Divide the beer-stock mixture among the 4 parcels, carefully pouring through the opening. Crimp the parcel closed tightly so that no liquid can escape. If you notice some leakage from the parcel, wrap it in a second layer of foil.

5. Heat the skillet or roasting pan over high heat. As they heat, the parcels will puff up. When this happens, place the skillet or roasting pan in the hot oven for 5 minutes.

6. Open or pierce the parcels at the table in front of the guests to allow the aromas to escape. If desired, serve with hollandaise sauce and/or small boiled potatoes. Neither is necessary, but they will add to the dish.

Note: State regulations for beer commerce vary, so monasteries rely on a network of local beer distributors. Look for Westmalle beer in fine liquor and grocery stores, or ask them to order it for you. You can also visit www.merchantduvin.com to find a Westmalle distributor near you.

ABBEY OF SAINT HILDEGARD

NEAR RÜDESHEIM, GERMANY

On any given Saturday half the town of Rüdesheim seems to be in this abbey's gift shop. Many come to taste the wines, which are poured by a nun in a flowing black habit, while another nun explains the store's unusual spelt products to customers. For those who prefer wine to spelt, the tasting room offers Rieslings that taste like ambrosia and look like bottled sunshine, brandies that please the eye as much as the palate, and liqueurs that breathe fire like a dragon. When the gift shop gets too crowded, one can step outside and drink in a scene that seems unchanged for a thousand years. Vineyards cover the steep slopes as far as the eye can see, while the Rhine glistens like a blue ribbon in the valley below. The pruning of the vines starts in late winter and lends the abbey an air of antici-pation that is almost palpable. Saint Hildegard would say that the earth is reclaiming its viridity, and a sip of the abbey's wine helps visitors do the same.

It's hard not to smile when one first encounters the nuns in the gift shop. They wear old-school Benedictine habits that announce in no uncertain terms that this abbey belongs to the Order of Saint Benedict. The Abbey of Saint Hildegard looks medieval, thanks to its soaring twin bell towers and imposing walls hewn of stone, but the church dates to 1900. Its voluminous form reminds one of the Cathedral of Trier—where Saint Hildegard once preached—while the frescoes inside have the sublime quality of a Piero della Francesca but actually belong to the Beuron School. The first nuns arrived in 1904 from the Abbey of Saint Gabriel in Prague; their family tree goes back much further—to a pair of monasteries founded by Saint Hildegard on either side of the Rhine, at Bingen in 1150 and Eibingen a few years later. (Guests on retreat can walk to Eibingen from Rüdesheim or check out the guidebooks in the gift shop for other great hiking trips.)

The nuns have a little more than six acres of vines, where they grow mostly Riesling and some Spätburgunder. They do everything from tending the vines to harvesting the grapes by hand and designing the lovely labels, which are based on miniatures that were painted by Saint Hildegard's nuns to illustrate her prolific writings. Two nuns are train-ing to be master vintners, so it's no surprise that the wines here are divine. The most popular ones are the trocken (dry) Domini, halbtrocken (half-dry) Sanctus, and Scivias (a little less dry than the others). Other top sellers are the abbey's Benedictus and Ange-lus wines (the angel on the latter label was designed by German artist Andreas Felger). For those who prefer beer, the gift shop carries a beer made with spelt, naturally, by monks at the Abbey of Plankstetten.

If one comes here knowing only one word of German, it might as well be *Dinkel*, or spelt. Saint Hildegard recommended spelt as a healthy grain back in the twelfth century, and the nuns here are experts on it. The shelves are lined with an unmatched variety of products made from this ancient grain: cookies (everything from biscotti to chocolate chip), crackers, pasta, bags of whole spelt, spelt flour, coffee, and more. It's a *Dinkel* lover's paradise. There are even spelt cookbooks, so there's no good reason not to try this grain even if it's new to one's diet. If the nuns are any indication, spelt must be good for you: the abbey has about fifty-five energetic nuns, of all ages, and one former abbess resigned only when she reached ninety.

It isn't easy to pick up Saint Hildegard's most famous work, *Scivias* (Know the Ways), and read it from scratch. This is due in part to the fact that Hildegard had the gift of divine visions, and the book was inspired by her muse, which she called the Living Light. Its religious language and themes can be opaque to secular readers, but there are passages whose message still speaks easily across the ages. When she says that the human intellect "sifts things as wheat is purified of any foreign matter, inquiring whether they are useful or useless, lovable or hateful, pertinent to life or death," it is as true today as it was in her time; try applying her definition of the intellect while watching TV and there's a good chance that less than one percent of what's on will still seem relevant.

It's much easier to get a sense of Saint Hildegard through her prolific letters to popes, emperors, archbishops, nuns, monks, and even ordinary folks, all of whom sought her prophetic insights and practical wisdom. In fact, Saint Hildegard was perhaps the only woman of her time who was both a cloistered nun and a sought-after public speaker. When she was more than sixty years old, she went on a preaching tour (her third) and took the clerics in Cologne to task for their self-indulgent behavior. It's amusing to read a letter from the clerics asking her for a copy of the sermon in which they say, "We were greatly astonished that God works through such a fragile sex, to display the great marvels of His secrets," and to see Saint Hildegard sign her reply with "Poor little timorous figure of a woman that I am," when in fact her scathing sermon must have had them all running for the confessional.

Hildegard also writes about something that she calls the tabernacle of the soul, a kind of house where reason, intellect, and will reside. She says that if someone gets angry, "gall is produced and brings the anger to its height by filling the tabernacle with smoke. If wicked delight rises up, the flame of lust touches its structure." It would be hard to find even one modern reader of this medieval visionary who can't relate to having a singed or sooty tabernacle. Still, Saint Hildegard was not one to sit in her ivory tower and make otherworldly pronouncements; she believed in an engaged Christian life and she usually offers a carrot with her stick, as when she says, "But there is another, lovely kind of joy, which is kindled in that tabernacle by the Holy Spirit, and the rejoicing soul receives it faithfully and perfects good works." Perhaps the best way to honor Saint Hildegard is to keep one's tabernacle tidy, listen to one's inner muse, and toast the nuns with a glass of Scivias.

FOOD PRODUCTS: Wine, liqueurs, spelt

GUESTHOUSE: Yes, M/F

WEBSITE: www.abtei-st-hildegard.de

ORDER: Phone, write, or use online form at
www.abtei-st-hildegard.de/klosterladen/klosterladen/kontakt.php

NOTE: For international calls, first dial 011 from the United States or 00 from
Europe, then 49 for Germany, followed by the local phone number listed
below; if the local number begins with a zero, drop it when dialing from
abroad.

PHONE: (0)6722/499-116

GUESTHOUSE E-MAIL: gaeste@abtei-st-hildegard.de

GUESTHOUSE PHONE: (0)6722/499-122

St. Hildegard Abbey
Postfach 1320, D—65378
Rüdesheim am Rhein
Germany

If you pass through Grand Central Terminal in New York, be sure to stop at wonderful Ciao Bella Gelato. You can cozy up to the high counter and eat heavenly gelato and sorbet while the rush-hour crowd whizzes by. One of the most unusual sorbets is made with wine, and Chef Danilo Zecchin kindly shared his recipe. He's from Italy, so you can thank him for this taste of la dolce vita.

1 pound fresh blackberries, rinsed, or thawed frozen blackberries

2 cups red wine, such as a light French burgundy (use Saint Hildegard's
    Spätburgunder if it is available; see Note)

¾ cup sugar

1 tablespoon fresh lemon juice

Mint leaves for garnish (optional)

1. If using fresh berries, reserve 4 for garnish and set aside. Purée the remaining blackberries in a blender. Strain through a fine-mesh sieve into a bowl, pressing firmly on the solids with the back of a spoon, and discard the seeds. Set aside.

2. Boil the wine in a small saucepan over medium-high heat until it reduces to 1 cup. Add 1 cup water and the sugar to the reduced wine and stir until completely dissolved. Stir in the blackberry purée and lemon juice and simmer for 2 to 3 minutes.

3. Transfer the sorbet base to a large metal bowl set over a water bath and let cool. Cover and place the sorbet base in the refrigerator for 1 hour, or until completely chilled.

4. Freeze the sorbet in an ice cream machine according to the manufacturer's instructions.

5. Scoop into 4 glasses or dessert dishes, garnish with fresh blackberries, if using, and mint leaves. Serve immediately.

Note: German Pinot Noirs like Saint Hildegard Spätburgunder are not widely available in the United States. A light French burgundy is a good substitute.

CHOCOLATE ESPRESSO CAKE   *Makes one 9-inch cake (8 servings)*

There is no better way to indulge one's inner muse than by whipping up this delightful spelt cake recipe, which has been adapted from www.Epicurious.com and Gourmet *magazine (October 2005). When measuring spelt flour, spoon it into the measuring cup and level it off to prevent packing it down; this helps keep the cake light.*

1½ sticks (¾ cup) unsalted butter, softened, plus additional for the pan

¾ cup unsweetened Dutch-process cocoa powder, plus additional for dusting
     the pan and cake

1 cup boiling-hot water

1½ tablespoons instant espresso powder

1½ teaspoons vanilla extract

1 teaspoon baking soda

½ pound Medjool dates (12 to 14), pitted and coarsely chopped (about 1½ cups)

2 cups spelt flour (see Note)

2 teaspoons baking powder

¾ teaspoon salt

1 cup packed dark brown sugar

2 large eggs

Lightly sweetened whipped cream (optional)

SPECIAL EQUIPMENT: 9-inch springform pan

1. Put the oven rack in the middle position and preheat the oven to 350°F. Butter the springform pan, then lightly dust with cocoa powder, knocking out excess.

2. Stir together the boiling-hot water, espresso powder, vanilla, and baking soda in a bowl, then add the dates, mashing lightly with a fork, and steep until the liquid cools to room temperature, about 10 minutes.

3. Whisk together the spelt flour, cocoa powder, baking powder, and salt in another bowl. Beat together the butter and brown sugar with an electric mixer at medium-high speed until pale and fluffy. Add the eggs 1 at a time, beating until just combined. Beat in the date mixture (the batter will look curdled), then reduce the speed to low and add the flour mixture, mixing until just combined.

4. Spoon the batter into the springform pan, smoothing the top, and bake until a wooden pick or skewer inserted into the center comes out clean, 50 minutes to 1 hour. Cool the cake in the pan on a rack for 5 minutes, then remove the side of the pan and cool the cake on a rack. Serve the cake warm or at room temperature with whipped cream, if you like.

Note: Saint Hildegard spelt is not currently available in the United States. Other brands of spelt flour can be found in health food stores and gourmet markets.

HOLY CHEESE

Cheese is milk's leap toward immortality.

—CLIFTON FADIMAN

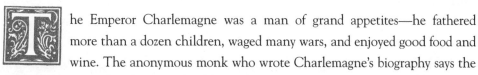

The Emperor Charlemagne was a man of grand appetites—he fathered more than a dozen children, waged many wars, and enjoyed good food and wine. The anonymous monk who wrote Charlemagne's biography says the Emperor first tasted a cheese with a bloomy rind at an abbey (the cheese was probably Brie or Roquefort). When he cut the rind away, one of the monks gently suggested that it was worth tasting. Charlemagne took a nibble and instantly became a fan; from then on, he had two cartloads of the cheese delivered to him every year.

Monks and nuns in Europe have made cheese since the Middle Ages. Until very recently, most monks were farmers and made cheese with milk from their own cows. Cheese was an important part of the vegetarian diet that was prescribed by Saint Benedict's rule, while extra cheese would have been sold or served to guests, just as it is today.

One of England's most famous cheeses, Wensleydale, owes its origins to the monks of Jervaulx Abbey in Yorkshire, who arrived from Normandy with William the Conqueror in the twelfth century. That tradition was abruptly ended when Henry VIII closed about eight hundred monasteries in England, Wales, and Ireland. Henry used rumors of bad monastic behavior (such as a pregnant nun and a monk who showed up drunk to Mass) to justify his actions, but those sins paled in comparison to his own. Despite the King's efforts, Yorkshire farmers remained loyal to the Catholic Church and still make Wensleydale cheese.

Charles de Gaulle once said of France that no one could be expected to rule a country with so many kinds of fromage. Of the five hundred or so cheeses that are made in France, some of the most famous owe their origins to monasteries: Maroilles was aged in cellars at the Abbey of Maroilles, Époisses was invented at the Abbey of Cîteaux, Bricquebec was named for Bricquebec Abbey, and the name Munster derives from the Latin word for "monastery." The French Revolution closed monasteries in France, but a monk in exile allegedly invented Camembert and others returned to France with new cheese-making skills.

The monks at the abbeys of Cîteaux in France and Westmalle in Belgium still make cheese with milk from their own cows, while monasteries such as Tamié in France and Gethsemani in the United States now buy milk from local producers. Other French monasteries that are worth a visit for their beauty as well as their fromage include the Abbey of Échourgnac in the Périgord, whose cheese is washed in a nut liqueur; Mont des Cats in French Flanders, where theirs is served with a good cup of coffee for breakfast, and Timadeuc in Brittany, whose cheese is a direct descendant of Port-du-Salut.

In Belgium, monks at the Abbey of Postel make an eponymous cheese that is delicious in *flamiche*, a dish from Flanders that is halfway between a quiche and a leek tart; pick up some cheese at the abbey for a picnic with Trappist beers, or stay for a retreat.

In the United States, the monks at Gethsemani are making cheese in unusual and innovative flavors, such as pesto (one of their best-sellers), while nuns at Our Lady of the Angels Monastery near Richmond, Virginia, make a cheese that has earned them the nickname "Gouda Girls."

Some abbeys, such as Tamié, age cheese in their own cellars, or caves. Others sell unripened cheese to an *affineur*, who ages the cheese to perfection. Cheese cellars provide specific temperature and humidity conditions for ripening cheeses; different caves may be used for cheese made with milk from goats, sheep, or cows. Some cheeses naturally develop a moldy rind, while others are washed in a salty brine to discourage mold.

The monks of Scourmont Abbey in Belgium sell a cheese that is washed with Chimay beer as it ripens. Chimay is a favorite cheese among some of New York's top cheese connoisseurs. James Coogan, manager of the Ideal Cheese Shop in Manhattan, says he likes to eat it on a slab of black bread with a cold glass of Chimay beer on the side (Chimay makes three beers that can be found in fine grocery and liquor stores in the United States). Waldemar Albrecht, *maître du fromage* at Artisanal Fromagerie & Bistro in Manhattan, suggests substituting Chimay for Reblochon in *tartiflette*, a delicious potato gratin dish from the Savoy region of France.

Beer and cheese go together at least as well if not better than wine and cheese. Brooklyn Brewery's brew master Garrett Oliver says this may be because beer uses grains (usually barley), and dairy animals also eat grains. He suggests pairing different kinds of monastery ales and cheese to see what you like, and when taste-testing cheese, remember to start with the mildest and work up to the strongest.

In France, cheese is often served with fresh fruit for dessert and is eaten with a knife and fork; if you are at an abbey in France or Belgium, do as the other guests do and use your utensils to eat the fromage. However, if you prefer your cheese with a slice of really good bread, try the Monks' Bread from Genesee Abbey in upstate New York, especially their sampler, which includes five flavors (www.monksbread.com). Or if you find yourself in France and prefer a picnic to a fancy cheese plate, swing by Sainte Madeleine in the Vaucluse for a magnificent loaf of freshly baked bread and pick up some wine at one of the region's numerous vineyards.

There are many ways one can visit French monasteries. An itinerary can focus on a particular region—say, the French Alps—or on one's favorite foods, such as cheese and chocolate. A sweet-toothed pilgrim in search of *pâtes de fruits* may wander as far north as Brittany and as far south as the Pyrenees, while less peripatetic folks can choose one city as a base and make day trips to several abbeys.

Cities that make good bases for day trips include Dijon for abbeys in Burgundy, Grenoble for abbeys in the French Alps, and Avignon or Marseilles for abbeys in and around Provence (the TGV from Paris to Marseilles puts one in the south quickly, where it's possible to rent a car or take buses and trains). Whichever route is chosen, rest assured that there is a perfect abbey for every palate.

SUGGESTED ITINERARY: THE CHEESE ROUTE

The great thing about visiting French abbeys that make cheese is that it's possible to start from almost any point in the country: the Abbey of Tamié is in the French Alps, Mont des Cats is in French Flanders, Timadeuc is in Brittany, and Échourgnac is in the Périgord. One can even swing north from Mont des Cats and head for the Abbey of Postel in Belgium (and drink Trappist beer along the way). The possibilities are endless and the cheese is superb.

TAMIÉ ABBEY (ABBAYE NOTRE-DAME DE TAMIÉ)

WWW.ABBAYE-TAMIE.COM

Tamié makes a cheese that is aged right beneath the abbey (the cheese cellars are not open to the public, but guests can purchase the cheese in the gift shop). The abbey's cheese looks a bit like Reblochon and tastes a tad like Tomme de Savoie, but it is truly unique. It is one of those foods—like cheese in Wisconsin or peaches in Georgia—that gives a place its identity, and the locals love it. American customers can find the abbey's cheese at fine grocers such as Dean & DeLuca or online at www.artisanalcheese.com.

MONT DES CATS ABBEY (ABBAYE DU MONT DES CATS)

WWW.ABBAYE-MONTDESCATS.FR

The abbey's eponymous cheese is a direct descendant of Port-du-Salut, a semisoft cheese with a mellow flavor and washed rind that was once made by monks at the Abbey of Notre-Dame du Port-du-Salut in Brittany; all true Trappist cheeses are made in a similar style. The monks who made Port-du-Salut helped other abbeys get back on their feet after the French Revolution by sharing their recipe, and Mont des Cats has made cheese ever since. Although the monks no longer milk their own cows, their cheese is still superb, and it's considered one of the culinary treasures of the Nord-Pas-de-Calais region.

The monks also have a bakery where they make cheese bread, naturally, and a regional specialty called *craquelin*—a brioche studded with pearl sugar. The abbey's baked goods are fit for angels, in part because the monks use flour that is milled for them at Oelenberg Abbey in Alsace.

TIMADEUC ABBEY (ABBAYE NOTRE-DAME DE TIMADEUC)

WWW.VANNES.CATHOLIQUE.FR

Note: This site is in French; use the search (*rechercher*) function and type in "Timadeuc."

Along with seafood, cider, and salted caramels, cheese from the Abbey of Timadeuc is one of the iconic foods of Brittany. One could argue that milk and butter simply taste better here than anywhere else, and it's certainly true with regards to the monks' cheese. The abbey's Timanoix cheese acquires its unforgettable flavor during aging, when the rind is washed with walnut liqueur. The monks also make a traditional Trappist cheese that is named after the abbey.

Pilgrims with a sweet tooth will find that the *pâtes de fruits* trail leads them to two abbeys in Brittany: Timadeuc, where it is made with apples from the monks' orchard, and the Monastery of Landévennec (aka Saint Guénolé), which is located on the banks of the lovely Aulne River (http://abbaye-landevennec.cef.fr); both abbeys welcome men and women for spiritual retreats.

ÉCHOURGNAC ABBEY
(ABBAYE NOTRE-DAME DE BONNE ESPÉRANCE)
WWW.ABBAYE-ECHOURGNAC.ORG

Walnuts are to the Périgord what butter is to Brittany—they are everywhere, and they are delicious. In a stroke of genius, the nuns of Échourgnac decided to wash the rind of their cheese in walnut liqueur. It's hard to describe exactly how this cheese tastes except to say that its smoky, nutty flavor seems to capture the very essence of the region's forests. The nuns also make a traditional Trappist cheese, *pâtes de fruits*, and jams.

Two things to keep in mind when visiting: The abbey's formal name is Our Lady of Good Hope, but it is commonly called Échourgnac, and the nuns don't speak much English, so be sure to brush up on your French before going. No trip to Échourgnac would be complete without a visit to the neighboring Benedictine priory of Saint Jean-Baptiste, where the monks make France's one and only monastery goat cheese.

When Julia Child chose twelve chefs to cook for her eightieth-birthday party, you knew the chefs had to be good. One of the chefs that Julia picked was Sanford "Sandy" D'Amato. Chef D'Amato shares a recipe here for flamiche, *a Flemish specialty that is halfway between a classic quiche and a leek tart. Foodies can catch Chef D'Amato's must-read column in the* Milwaukee Journal Sentinel *or visit his award-winning restaurant in Milwaukee.*

PASTRY

    1¾ cups all-purpose flour

    7 tablespoons cold unsalted butter, cut into small dice

    Pinch of salt

    1 egg, separated

FILLING

    2 thick-cut bacon slices (about 3 ounces), cut in ¼-inch pieces

    1 small leek (about 6 ounces), white and light green parts only, trimmed, split
        lengthwise, washed, and cut on the diagonal in ¼-inch-thick slices

    Salt and freshly ground black pepper

    1 whole egg

    ½ egg yolk (reserved from the tart shell)

    Pinch of freshly grated nutmeg

    6 tablespoons sour cream

    ½ cup heavy cream

    ½ cup whole milk

    5 ounces Postel cheese (see Note), or Raclette or Morbier, diced

SPECIAL EQUIPMENT: 1-inch-deep round 10-inch tart pan with a removable bottom

1. For the pastry: Put the flour, butter, and salt into a food processor and pulse 10 to 15 times, until the mixture is flecked with pea-size bits of butter. Take half of the egg yolk (reserve the remaining half for the filling) and mix with 4½ tablespoons cold water. Turn the machine on and pour the mixture in quickly through the hole in the lid. When a ball just starts to form, stop the food processor—do not overwork. Remove the dough, form into a ball, and dust lightly with flour. Flatten the dough into a disk, wrap in plastic wrap, and refrigerate at least 1 hour or overnight.

2. Roll the dough out on a lightly floured surface into a 14-inch round, then ease into a 10-inch tart pan, making sure dough is snugly fit in the crease of the pan. Refrigerate the shell for at least 30 minutes.

3. Preheat the oven to 375°F. Remove the shell from the refrigerator, trim excess dough from the edges, and cover the pastry with a piece of aluminum foil or parchment paper (lightly pressed into the crease of the pan); fill with dried beans or rice on top to weigh down. Bake for 12 to 15 minutes, until the sides are set and just starting to color. Reduce the heat to 350°F, remove the foil with the beans or rice, and continue to bake until lightly golden and cooked but not too brown, about 10 minutes. Check the tart crust occasionally for puffing; press down lightly with a clean cloth every 3 minutes if the pastry puffs up. Remove from the oven and leave the oven on. Beat the egg white, then brush it inside the tart shell (you do not have to use all of the egg white). Cool to room temperature.

4. For the filling: Cook the bacon in a nonstick medium pan over medium heat until just golden. Add the leeks to the bacon, season with salt and pepper, and cook, stirring to coat well, until the leeks are crisp-tender, about 2 minutes. Spread the bacon-leek mixture onto a plate to cool.

5. Beat the egg and reserved yolk half, 1 teaspoon salt, a pinch of pepper,

and the nutmeg in a medium bowl. Add the sour cream and blend until smooth. Slowly whisk in the cream and milk until well combined. Place the tart pan on a cookie sheet. Scatter half of the bacon-leek mixture and cheese on the bottom of the tart crust, then pour in half of the custard mixture. Add the remaining bacon-leek mixture and the cheese.

6. Put the tart pan on a cookie sheet and place on the oven rack. Pour enough custard in the tart shell to come up to the top of the edge of the shell, but do not overfill. Bake until just set, about 25 minutes. Remove from the oven and let rest on a rack for at least 15 minutes, then serve. The *flamiche* can be reheated in 325°F oven.

Note: Postel is not yet widely available in the United States; however, Raclette and Morbier are good substitutes and both can be purchased at www.artisanalcheese.com.

Sister Myriam, who manages a website for Trappist abbeys in France at www .monastic-euro.org, shared this delicious recipe. It uses fresh goat cheese made by the monks of Saint Jean-Baptiste Priory. You can substitute another goat cheese if the priory's cheese proves hard to find.

4 golden apples

6 tablespoons unsalted butter

2 tablespoons vanilla sugar (see Notes)

8 leaves thawed (9 × 14-inch sheets) phyllo dough

⅓ cup golden raisins

4 ounces Saint Jean-Baptiste Priory fresh goat cheese (see Notes) or other fresh
   goat cheese, ash or rind removed, cut into small cubes

½ tablespoon sugar

½ tablespoon hazelnut oil (optional)

1. Peel the apples, core, and cut each into 8 wedges. Melt 3½ tablespoons of the butter in a nonstick skillet over medium-high heat. Add the apples, sprinkle with the vanilla sugar, and cook, tossing occasionally, until golden brown, 8 to 10 minutes. Transfer to a colander set over a bowl to drain.

2. Preheat the oven to 350°F. Melt the remaining butter and lightly grease a disposable or metal 9-inch round aluminum pie pan. Arrange 1 sheet of phyllo dough in the center of the pie pan, brush lightly with some butter, then lay another sheet on top crosswise. (Keep the remaining phyllo leaves moist by covering them with a sheet of plastic wrap and then a damp cloth.) Repeat the layering and buttering of phyllo with 2 more sheets of phyllo, rotating the phyllo so the entire pan is covered.

3. Scatter the raisins, then the well-drained apples, and then cubes of cheese over the phyllo. Pull the edges of the dough up over the apple mixture, tamp down well, and cover the pie with 4 more sheets of phyllo dough, assembling as before, lightly brushing each layer with butter and layering crosswise and rotated so entire pan is covered. (You may not need all of the butter.) Lightly cover the pie with another pie pan and gently invert so the ends of the phyllo can be pulled over and smoothed on the top of the pie to make a compact disk. Again, cover the pie with the other pie pan and invert again to the smoother side of the pie. Brush some more butter over the top of the pie and sprinkle with the sugar.

4. Bake until phyllo is golden, about 30 minutes. Transfer the pie to a wire rack for 30 to 60 minutes to cool. Sprinkle the warm pie with hazelnut oil, if using, and then serve immediately.

Notes: To make your own vanilla sugar, split a vanilla bean lengthwise, then scrape the seeds out and mix into 2 cups of granulated sugar. Bury the bean into the sugar, seal tightly, and store for 1 to 2 weeks before using.

Saint Jean-Baptiste Priory's cheese is not currently available in the United States, but you can substitute it with your favorite fresh goat cheese.

SUGGESTED ITINERARY: A TASTE OF PROVENCE

The abbeys of Provence are some of the most peaceful and lovely in the world. They are within easy driving distance of each other and pilgrims of both the spiritual and culinary sort can add other abbeys in the south of France to their itineraries.

The following is a suggestion for one itinerary that introduces visitors to an excellent sample of what the region has to offer. Technically speaking, two out of three of these abbeys are not in Provence: Aiguebelle is in the Drôme Provençale—or, as the monks like to say, it's "on the doorstep of Provence"—while Sainte Madeleine is in the Vaucluse, but Provence is already in the air.

AIGUEBELLE ABBEY (ABBAYE NOTRE-DAME D'AIGUEBELLE)
WWW.ABBAYE-AIGUEBELLE.COM

There's something about the way light bounces off Aiguebelle's white stone walls that makes the abbey seem as if it were made of honey-spun nougat. The place simply glows. The land here is rugged—scented with pine, carved with rivers, and studded with chalky-white rocks—but one still senses that this is the threshold of Provence. Lizards dart underfoot, sprays of brilliant orange flowers cling to rocky ledges, and fields of lavender line the hiking trails. It's an invigorating place, and the monks make an equally invigorating elixir. Alexion is made with a whole garden's worth of herbs, but it tastes refreshing rather than medicinal. It's available in the abbey's excellent gift shop.

Just remember to pack a bottle or two of Alexion for the road. There's nothing better for calming a stomach that has overindulged in nougat. Try to practice monastic restraint while visiting the amazing artisanal nougat shops in Nyons, Montélimar, and other towns throughout the Drôme Provençale.

SAINTE MADELEINE ABBEY
(ABBAYE SAINTE-MADELEINE DU BARROUX)
WWW.BARROUX.ORG

Lavender fields surround this abbey, which looks deceptively ancient but was built in modern times (in an unusual twist of fate, this contemporary abbey—which was funded with donations from a conservative wing of the church—practices ancient traditions such as wearing tonsures and chanting a Latin liturgy; women are not accepted in the guesthouse but the monks can provide a list of local hotels). Regardless of its relative youth, the abbey is beautiful. Come here for Sainte Madeleine's rustic loaves of bread, delicious *pâte d'amandes*, and wine from the monastery's vineyard.

Best of all, the Vaucluse is a biker's paradise. If you bike to the abbey, be sure to dress respectfully. Then load a backpack with picnic food and hit the trails—there are miles of them. Bike maps are available at the tourist office in Beaumes-de-Venise.

GANAGOBIE ABBEY (ABBAYE NOTRE-DAME DE GANAGOBIE)
WWW.NDGANAGOBIE.COM

Olive oil, honey-flavored *pâtes de fruits*, and hand lotions scented with lavender and other herbs are only a few of the reasons to visit this abbey. It's undoubtedly one of the most charming places in the Alpes-de-Haute-Provence, and it draws guests from Marseilles and even as far away as Paris. However, the monks speak only French and the guesthouse is often booked, so feel free to make this a day trip if necessary. Be sure to look for Ganagobie's mascot, a medieval elephant, in the fantastic mosaics on the floor of the church.

Steven Jenkins is master cheesemonger at Fairway markets in Manhattan and Red Hook, Brooklyn, where savvy shoppers flock in droves for the fresh produce and the world-class cheese counter. Jenkins is also the author of *A Cheese Primer*, a must-read addition to any foodie's bookshelf. Steve shared these tips for selecting and buying the best monastery cheese.

The thing about cheese (and beer and wine, of course) made by monks and nuns—whether they are Benedictine, Cistercian, Franciscan, or one of several other ancient orders—is that so many of them have become victims of their own success.

You can imagine the following that would occur for a tender, succulent, alluringly smelly cheese that has been found in local and not-so-local markets for a generation or two; or as is the case with, say, Port-du-Salut (the original Trappist cheese), something like six generations (since circa 1850). Suddenly the demand for the cheese is such that its production becomes overwhelmingly labor-intensive, and the accounting for the business of it is simply more than a monastery can handle. The result is that the monastery allows the cheese to be "farmed out," that is, made by a cheesemaking specialist whose aim is to produce and sell as much cheese as his physical plant will allow, and we all know what that means.

The cheese loses its rusticity, its cachet, its complex and mesmerizing flavor and fragrance, simply because it has lost its link to the nuns' fingers and elbows and breath, to the monks' sweet and miraculous raw milk and even sweeter coddled cattle, each given a name rather than a number.

Cheese made from pasteurized (dead) milk, and even worse, made in great quantities, cannot be memorable cheese. Commercially successful, yes—but not memorable. Port-Salut (the "du" has been lost) and

Saint-Paulin, another unprotected name, are among the most forgettable cheeses made, both having origins in monastic orders. Quebecois Oka is another once great cheese formerly made by monks that has been vitiated by its own success.

So I urge you to seek out those that have not yet succumbed—Échourgnac from the Périgord region of France (available at Fairway markets), Mont des Cats from Flanders, and Chimay from Belgium.

Several of the world's greatest cheeses survived their passage from religious-order origins to the secular world of cheesemaking. Munster d'Alsace and its close cousin Géromé, and Burgundian Époisses are still excruciatingly delicious.

CÎTEAUX ABBEY

NEAR DIJON IN THE CÔTE-D'OR (BURGUNDY), FRANCE

It's hard to refrain from gluttony in this part of France. It's even harder when one discovers that this abbey, one of the most famous in the history of monasticism, is within driving distance of Dijon. The last hope of avoiding overindulgence evaporates when one walks into the fromagerie run by Alain Hess in nearby Beaune. The shop stocks cheese made with every kind of milk and aged to perfection. Spiritual pilgrims can console themselves for giving in to their appetites by making sure to buy fromage made by the monks of Cîteaux; pick up some good bread and sparkling lemon juice to go with the cheese and have a picnic on the way to the abbey. *C'est la vie en rose!*

Monks are fond of saying that monastic life is full of paradoxes, and Cîteaux is no exception—it's an ancient abbey with a brand-new church, and in a place where Saint Bernard became a monk in his early twenties it's odd to see teenagers playing ball on the lawn. The Abbey of Cîteaux was founded in 1098 by Saint Robert, with help from Saints Alberic and Stephen Harding, and it is the motherhouse of the Cistercian Order; a seventeenth-century reform at the Abbey of La Trappe gave rise to the Order of Cistercians of the Strict Observance, whose members go by the nickname Trappists.

When Robert and his small band of monks struck out for what was then a swampy patch of land punctuated by cattails, they left behind the Monastery of Molesmes, where large donations had paradoxically rendered the community lazy and self-indulgent. The monks who bravely walked out into the wilderness to found their new abbey may not have been aware of it at the time, but they were about to plant the seeds of one of the greatest monastic reformations of all time. At the center of that reformation was a desire to live a life in strict accordance with the Rule of Saint Benedict.

Modern consumers could learn a lot from the ascetic example of the ancient Desert Fathers and the medieval monks of Cîteaux, but it's never easy for people to give up a life of luxury. That was true as much in Saint Robert's day as it is now, and in its early years the new monastery struggled to find recruits. Then a spiritual thunderbolt struck Cîteaux: Saint Bernard arrived with thirty-one of Burgundy's finest noblemen in tow. It's hard to imagine the impact one person can have in the short span of a lifetime, but the numbers tell a remarkable story. There were only a handful of monks at Cîteaux when Bernard decided to join, but by the time of his death there were seven hundred monks living at Clairvaux alone—an abbey founded by Bernard—and more than one hundred Trappist abbeys throughout Europe.

Staying in Dijon is a day-tripper's best bet since there isn't an enormous choice of things to do on the abbey's grounds, but beware that driving in Dijon is a nightmare for the uninitiated (study a map closely before arriving and choose a hotel on a main road to avoid losing one's sanity while navigating the medieval quarter). On the other hand, any young man who wants to explore a vocation or simply do a retreat will find that this is an excellent abbey for spiritual reflection, and the community includes some young monks who are very welcoming. Just be prepared for the crowds of Europeans who paradoxically arrive in their BMWs and Mercedes-Benzes.

Day-trippers and other guests can take a contemplative walk along the path that leads past the lovely rose garden and is paved with a series of round stones that tell the history of the Cistercians in charming detail. Then head for the gift shop to sample cheese and buy products from other monasteries. Tours of the grounds are available from May through early October and visitors are always welcome to join the monks for daily prayers.

The Abbey of Cîteaux once owned about 10,000 acres of land, including some of Burgundy's finest vineyards, such as Clos Romanée. The abbey's lands were seized as government property during the French Revolution and the monks were exiled. The

Cistercians returned in 1898 and began making Abbaye de Cîteaux cheese in 1925. Cîteaux is sometimes credited with inventing another great cheese, Époisses, which is no longer made by monks but is still divine; Cîteaux and Époisses can be found in better cheese shops in the United States and Europe. Look for a version of Saint Benedict's dictum, *Prière & Travail* (prayer and work), on the abbey's cheese wrapper.

Cîteaux is made with raw milk from the monk's herd of Montbéliard cows, a brown-and-white breed that is to northern France and Switzerland what Holsteins are to America's dairyland. The monks have their own cheese caves and their cheese is also aged by master cheese-monger Alain Hess in Beaune, who sells it when it reaches its prime, at about three weeks old. It's hard to think of a better way to spend a day near Dijon than visiting the abbey in the morning, attending prayers at noon, and spending the afternoon enjoying cheese and wine in Beaune.

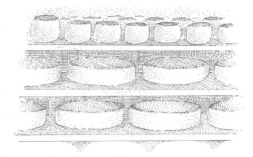

Bernard was so persuasive and his vocation was so fervent that many young men chose to follow him. No less than one uncle and four brothers immediately followed him into monastic life. Legend has it that as Bernard and his kin prepared to depart for Cîteaux, they told the one remaining brother that he would inherit the entire family estate. The brother complained that this was an unfair deal and that they were taking heaven with them and leaving him only earthly possessions; eventually he also became a monk. While times have changed and families, Catholic and otherwise, are now smaller, Bernard's example can still inspire the right young man to follow in his footsteps. Perhaps the path will lead him to Cîteaux to stay.

FOOD PRODUCTS: Cheese

GUESTHOUSE: Yes, M/F

WEBSITE: www.citeaux-abbaye.com

ORDER: Cîteaux can be found at the abbey gift shop, and in fine cheese shops in Dijon and Paris. It is not currently available in the United States.

E-MAIL: visites@citeaux-abbaye.com (for guided tours)

NOTE: For international calls, first dial 011 from the United States or 00 from Europe, then 33 for France, followed by the local phone number listed below; if the local number begins with a zero, drop it when dialing from abroad.

PHONE: (0)3 80 61 34 28

GUESTHOUSE E-MAIL: hotelier@citeaux-abbaye.com

GUESTHOUSE PHONE: (0)3 80 61 35 34

Cîteaux Abbey

21700 Saint-Nicolas-lès-Cîteaux

TAMIÉ ABBEY

NEAR ALBERTVILLE IN SAVOY, FRANCE

Once upon a time there was a French abbot who lived at a small Trappist abbey in Africa. One day a young man showed up who said he was thinking of becoming a monk. The young man was also from France, where all the abbeys he had seen were too large for his liking. He told the abbot he wanted to join an abbey that was small, youthful, beautiful—and used more French than Latin. The abbot thought this was a bit like finding Goldilocks just the right bed, but he finally came up with the perfect place: the Abbey of Tamié. Now, the young man had heard that Tamié sits in a pretty valley and anyone who sees it in summer is sure to fall in love—so he went there in the dead of winter to test his mettle. He's still at Tamié, and guests can thank him for making the retreat house so comfortable that they will wish they never had to leave.

The Abbey of Tamié was founded by Saint Peter of Tarentaise in 1132. It belongs to the Order of Cistercians of the Strict Observance (Trappists) and was founded not long after Cîteaux. The abbey is tucked into a halcyon valley dotted with alpine meadows and woods and ringed by the peaks of the Bauges Massif. This is the Savoy, a region of France that is as famous for cheese as it is for hosting the 1992 Olympics in Albertville. In fact, the Olympics and skiing in general have made this region so popular that even this secluded monastery couldn't avoid detection; guests must book a retreat far in advance, but be patient—it's worth it. The monks are as famous for their music as they are for their cheese.

Saint Benedict said, "Listen . . . with the ear of your heart" ("*Écoute . . . ouvre l'oreille de ton coeur*"). If one learns to listen that way, the music here will open one's heart to God. The monks are famous for their musical talents and also for singing mostly in French rather than Latin. It's the French liturgy—along with the cheese, good company, and chalet-style guesthouse—that makes this one of the most welcoming abbeys for guests on retreat. The present church was begun in 1679 and has wonderful acoustics and rugged stone walls that feel protective rather than fierce. It is a lovely place to hear the monks sing, especially at Compline before heading to bed; don't be surprised if you find yourself humming the Canticle of Simeon or Salve Regina as you nod off to sleep.

With all due respect to Saint Benedict, one can also listen with the ear of one's stomach! There is a simple but profound pleasure to be had in nibbling on a slice of Tamié cheese with a glass of unpretentious red wine in the dining room, while gazing out on a mountain view that would feel right at home in *The Sound of Music*. This is surely some of the freshest cheese a visitor will ever taste. It's no wonder, since the monks use only fresh whole milk from farms in the valley where cows graze on alpine meadows in summer and hay in winter. Even the cows here are picturesque, but don't be fooled into thinking they are frail; these brown and white Tarentaise and Abondance breeds happily munch their way up slopes where Holsteins fear to tread.

In a wonderful twist on traditional abbey architecture, the monks age the cheese for up to one month in caves that lie below the cloister. Like many abbeys in the Middle Ages, the monks first made cheese for their own consumption. They used to make a cheese like Port-du-Salut—the original Trappist washed-rind cheese—but that recipe was lost when soldiers forced the monks to leave during the French Revolution. This turned out to be a lucky thing for cheese lovers; today cheese aficionados will say that Tamié most closely resembles Reblochon or Tomme de Savoie, but it has a taste all its own and is pretty to boot, with a saffron-colored rind that develops a slight bloom during aging.

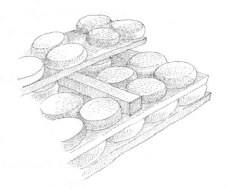

Tamié cheese is found throughout the Savoy region and at better cheese shops in Paris. Visitors can stock up on the abbey's cheese and CDs at the gift shop just down the road from the guesthouse, which also sells CDs by jazz singers such as Bessie Smith (one of the monks here must have liked jazz), a wide selection of children's books, and food from other monasteries.

This abbey is particularly well suited to artists, writers, and composers who need a quiet place to think but who also enjoy the camaraderie of coffee after a hearty meal. (Keep in mind that French is the lingua franca here, and almost no one speaks English; it's a good idea to brush up on a few French phrases before you go.) The abbey is perched at 3,000 feet and is blissfully free of the highways and urban sprawl that have begun to plague some monasteries. While Tamié has no extensive hiking trails, short walks are possible along a well-paved road that runs past a pretty waterfall. There is no reason to rush here. A tiny wild strawberry making its unlikely debut in October can speak to a hiker as much of God as the massive mountain to which it clings.

As a visitor to Tamié recently prepared to depart, she remarked to a nun who also happened to be leaving that day that she had never felt a greater sense of peace than she had as a guest here. The nun said that the best way to keep the spirit of Tamié in one's heart is to take the abbey's CDs home and listen to them with closed eyes, and no matter where one is, one will be transported back to Tamié. In other words, learn to listen to these monks with the ear of your heart and the Abbey of Tamié will continue to speak to you long after you leave.

FOOD PRODUCTS: Cheese

GUESTHOUSE: Yes, M/F

WEBSITE: www.abbaye-Tamie.com

ORDER: Tamié can be found in the abbey gift shop and at fine cheese stores and grocery stores in France and the United States (see Shopping Guide).

E-MAIL: sotam@abbaye-Tamie.com (for general inquiries)

NOTE: For international calls, first dial 011 from the United States or 00 from Europe, then 33 for France, followed by the local phone number listed below; if the local number begins with a zero, drop it when dialing from abroad.

PHONE: (0)4 79 31 15 52 (abbey store)

FAX: (0)4 79 37 05 24

GUESTHOUSE E-MAIL: accueil@abbaye-Tamie.com

Tamié Abbey

Plancherine 73200 Albertville, Savoy

France

In the Savoy region of France the locals like to infuse Tamié with the flavor of truffles (they also like to infuse Brie in a similar manner). This recipe comes from Laure Dubouloz, who works with Hervé Mons, one of France's finest affineurs. Laure grew up near the Abbey of Tamié. She says the abbey's cheese was originally served this way by the chef at the restaurant Le Gay Séjour in Faverges. Laure's father, Jacques Dubouloz, who is an affineur in Annecy, adapted the recipe and sold it during the holiday season. Serve with a glass of Champagne!

1 wheel (about 1½ pounds) Abbaye de Tamié (see Notes), not too aged, chilled
(the cheese will slice easier if it's well chilled)
1 black truffle (see Notes), preferably from Savoy

Slice the wheel of cheese in half horizontally so you have 2 equal portions. Shave the truffle very thinly with a truffle slicer or mandoline, sprinkling the shavings evenly over one portion of the cheese to cover it completely. Reassemble the cheese and wrap it tightly in plastic wrap. Place the cheese in a container with a tight lid and let it sit in the refrigerator for 10 days. Unwrap and serve with bread or crackers.

Notes: Visit www.artisanalcheese.com to purchase Abbaye de Tamié.

Black truffles can be purchased from www.gourmetfoodstore.com. Purchase whichever kind of truffle—black or white, winter or summer, fresh or frozen—that your purse can manage.

A secular cheese expert who works with the monks shared this recipe for a rustic grilled cheese sandwich that is eaten by the locals in Savoy, who are especially fond of the abbey's cheese. If you can't find Tamié, try Reblochon or a similar cheese. Serve with a small salad for a light meal. The abbey's cheese pairs well with white or red wines from the Savoy region.

1 slice country bread

½ to 1 teaspoon white wine, preferably from the Savoy region

1 or 2 slices Abbaye de Tamié (see Note)

Preheat the oven to 450°F. Place the bread on a baking sheet. Lightly sprinkle some of the wine on the bread, being careful not to soak the bread. Top the bread with the cheese and bake until cheese is nice and melted, five to seven minutes. Let cool slightly before eating.

Note: Visit www.artisanalcheese.com to purchase Abbaye de Tamié.

Browned Sole with Shrimp, Gnocchi, and Abbaye de Tamié

If you are going to splurge on only one extraordinary meal in Paris, Taillevent is a wonderful choice. Chef Alain Solivérès kindly shared this elegant recipe, which has been adapted here for the home cook. If you want to taste the original version, made with crayfish, you'll have to pay your respects to Chef Solivérès in person on your next trip to France and hope that it is on the menu. In the meantime, this adapted version is still fit for angels.

Note that the gnocchi recipe yields about twice as much as you will need for this dish. Freeze the remainder in a single layer on a sheet pan, then transfer to a resealable plastic bag or container and use them later for another meal.

GNOCCHI

¾ cup water

6 tablespoons unsalted butter

½ teaspoon salt

¾ cup all-purpose flour, sifted

2 to 3 eggs

2 basil leaves, finely chopped

GARNISH

¼ cup olive oil

12 large shrimp, shelled and deveined, tail on

12 chanterelles, stems trimmed and scraped

3 thin slices prosciutto

3 tablespoons finely chopped garlic

3 tablespoons finely chopped parsley

1 medium shallot, minced

1.5 ounces *glace de poulet* (see Notes), diluted with ¼ cup water

SOLE

4 (5 to 6 ounces each) sole fillets

1½ ounces Abbaye de Tamié (see Notes), rind trimmed and cheese cut into small
pieces

3 tablespoons softened unsalted butter

¾ cup dried bread crumbs

¼ cup lobster bisque, warmed

2 teaspoons whipped cream

1. For the gnocchi: Bring the water, butter, and salt to a boil in a medium pot over medium-high heat and boil until the butter melts. Remove from the heat. Add the flour all at once, stirring vigorously with a wooden spoon until a glossy dough forms and pulls away from the sides and bottom of the pot and forms a ball. Transfer the dough to the bowl of a standing mixer and cool for 5 minutes.

2. Meanwhile, bring a wide pot of salted water to a boil. Add 2 of the eggs to the dough, 1 at a time, beating until the egg is thoroughly incorporated before adding the next. If the batter is very stiff and does not slide off of a rubber spatula after the second egg, add the third egg. Add the basil and stir well.

3. Reduce the heat to maintain the water at a simmer; do not allow it to boil. Working in batches of about 20 gnocchi at a time, drop the batter by small spoonfuls into the pot of water. The gnocchi will fall to the bottom of the pot and then float to the top. Allow them to cook for another 3 minutes after they float to the

top. Using a slotted spoon, transfer the gnocchi to a sheet pan lined with paper towels or a lint-free towel as they are done. Allow the water to return to a simmer before you drop in the next batch. The recipe should yield 45 to 50 gnocchi. Set 20 aside, then freeze the rest for another meal.

4. For the garnish: Heat 2 tablespoons of the olive oil in a large nonstick pan. Add the gnocchi and sauté until golden. Meanwhile, in a separate large skillet, heat the remaining oil until hot, then add the shrimp and mushrooms and sauté. When the shrimp are almost cooked through, add the prosciutto, garlic, parsley, and shallots. Cook for another minute, then add the gnocchi to the skillet. Deglaze the pan with the *glace de poulet* and set aside in a warm place.

5. For the sole: Preheat the broiler. Arrange the sole fillets in a single layer on an aluminum foil–lined baking sheet. Broil for 3 minutes. Meanwhile, mash the cheese, butter, and bread crumbs together with your fingers to form a paste-like mixture. Turn the fish over and drop the cheese mixture in coarse crumbs over the fish. Broil until the crumb mixture turns golden and the fish is cooked through, about 2 minutes.

6. To serve, divide the garnish among 4 plates. Spoon the lobster bisque over the garnish, then top with the whipped cream. Place the fish on top of the garnish, and serve immediately.

Notes: More Than Gourmet produces a *glace de poulet* that can be purchased directly from www.morethangourmet.com or at gourmet grocers.

Visit www.artisanalcheese.com to purchase Abbaye de Tamié.

ABBEY OF GETHSEMANI

NEAR BARDSTOWN, KENTUCKY

Monks generally are spared the worst excesses of our 24/7, consumer-driven society, but what escape is there for the layperson? A good place to seek answers is at the Abbey of Gethsemani, as famous for the writings of Thomas Merton as it is for cheese, fruitcake, and bourbon fudge. Gethsemani was founded in 1848 by monks from Melleray Abbey in France and belongs to the Order of Cistercians of the Strict Observance (aka Trappists). Locals call this part of Kentucky "The Holy Land" because so many Catholics came here from Ireland and Maryland in the eighteenth century, fleeing England's anti-Catholic penal laws. This is also bourbon country, and one of the best places to taste Kentucky bourbon is at the Old Talbott Tavern in Bardstown, whose famous visitors have included Abraham Lincoln, Jesse James, Daniel Boone, and James Audubon.

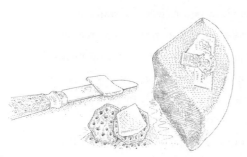

Gethsemani once made cheese with milk from its own herd of prizewinning Holsteins. That was easier to do when there were more than two hundred monks living here, as there were after World War II. Today the monks buy milk from local producers, but their cheese is still wonderful. The pesto flavor is a customer favorite and goes well with crackers, as does the mild. There are also smoked and aged varieties. Armchair travelers can shop for cheese on the Gethsemani Farms website but should keep in mind that the abbey doesn't ship cheese in the hottest summer months.

Kentucky winters can be surprisingly cold, and there's no better way to beat the chill than with a taste of bourbon. Fortunately, the monks make two flavors of fudge, chocolate pecan and butter walnut, with enough bourbon in them to put a southern drawl in even a Yankee's speech. Bourbon fans will think they have died and gone to heaven when they taste it (but kids don't like it as much as adults do, so remember to use the abbey's whiskey-free fudge as a stocking stuffer for the little ones).

The monks also soak their fruitcake in bourbon. Rest assured, this is not the infamous fruitcake of doorstop jokes. Gethsemani's cake is so good that *The Wall Street Journal* once rated it "best overall" in a fruitcake taste test. Just think of it as a spice cake studded with the perfect amount of fruit rather than a dried fruit cocktail run amok and made even drier by powdered sugar. Served with a cup of coffee and perhaps a dollop of whipped cream, Gethsemani's version of this classic holiday treat will have guests asking for second helpings.

Fudge, fruitcake, and cheese are joyful indulgences whose consequences are mainly caloric. But where is a layperson to turn for spiritual nourishment in a culture more interested in the latest celebrity breakups than in confronting life's real challenges? Do individual thoughts still matter in a world that prizes relentless action and mindless consumption? Gethsemani is a good place to contemplate how best to feed the soul.

A visitor to Gethsemani can't help noticing that guests on retreat are reading. They read in their rooms, on the terrace, and in the garden. They read during meals, after Mass, and before Vespers. There is no rule that requires reading, nor any need to suggest it: *lectio divina*, or meditative reading of spiritual books, simply blossoms in the silence. Along with work and prayer, spiritual reading is one of the pillars of monastic life according to Saint Benedict's rule; it's also a good way for laypersons to train their minds on retreat and at home.

Some visitors read Thomas Merton, whose memoir, *The Seven Storey Mountain*, tells the story of his conversion. He describes how he went from an agnostic and peripatetic life in Europe and America to making vows at Gethsemani. Another good read is Merton's *No Man Is an Island*, which at least one monk at Gethsemani credits with influencing his decision to join the monastery. Merton was a bridge builder between spiritual people and was interested in Eastern spiritual traditions; both the Dalai Lama and Thich Nhat Hanh came to Gethsemani to meet him. Guests will find books by each of them in the abbey gift shop, and they can even pay their respects at Merton's grave, which lies in a part of the cemetery that is outside the monastic enclosure and can be visited.

Other guests read Saint Bernard, whose medieval descriptions of human nature, and especially of the many guises of pride, are so accurate and so timeless that a modern reader can still recognize a falsely humble boss or backstabbing colleague in Bernard's words. The notion that spiritual growth is a process is one that Bernard wholly embraces, and he recommends meditation, prayer, and finally contemplative prayer like that practiced by the monks as progressive steps toward a richer spiritual life. This should hearten any beginner for whom an inner life is still a new concept.

Saint Hildegard offers readers a more mystical twist on *lectio divina*. She was a visionary, composer, and keen observer of nature who developed many home health remedies, although her approach to medicine was strictly medieval. As a cure for dry eyes, she suggests opening them wide while staring at an emerald-green field as though to soak up its verdant moisture. This may not work, but it's a lovely thought. A more modern remedy might include closing one's eyes and meditating to Hildegard's music.

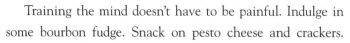

Training the mind doesn't have to be painful. Indulge in some bourbon fudge. Snack on pesto cheese and crackers. Serve fruitcake to a friend. Then try turning off the TV (have more fudge if this step proves difficult). Next, pick up a book that gives your soul something to chew on.

Fans of the monastery's fudge would never guess that Gethsemani got its start by making wine and curing ham. However, the monks eventually decided that it wasn't entirely appropriate for vegetarian monks to be selling meat, and they began looking for other ways to earn a living. Meanwhile, one of the monks was experimenting with a cheese recipe that he had brought back from a trip to France; the other monks liked the idea of making cheese, and what began as one monk's hobby soon turned into a full-fledged fromage factory. When there were more than two hundred monks at Gethsemani, as was the case right after World War II, the monastery had enough manpower to care for its own prizewinning herd of Holsteins. Today the monks get their milk from local producers. In addition to cheese, they make a tasty fruitcake and their famous bourbon fudge.

FOOD PRODUCTS: Cheese, fudge, fruitcake

GUESTHOUSE: Yes, M/F

WEBSITE: www.monks.org

ORDER: E-mail, phone, or write

E-MAIL: gethfarms@monks.org

PHONE: 800-549-0912 (toll-free)

GUESTHOUSE PHONE: 502-549-4133, 8:00 a.m. to noon, except Sundays

(Reservations must be made by phone.)

Abbey of Gethsemani

Gethsemani Farms

3642 Monks Road

Trappist, KY 40051-6102

What could be more fun than a crunchy, cheesy cauliflower fritter made with mon-astery cheese? Only a monk could dream up such a delicious combination that's also easy to make. This recipe is adapted from Brother Victor-Antoine d'Avila-Latourrette's book From a Monastery Kitchen: The Classic Natural Foods Cookbook.

1 egg, lightly beaten

¾ cup whole milk

¾ cup all-purpose flour

¾ cup (about 1 ounce) finely grated Gethsemani cheese (see Note) or other
     Trappist-style cheese

Salt

1 small head cauliflower, trimmed of leaves

Canola or vegetable oil for deep-frying

1. Whisk the egg and milk together in a large bowl. Add the flour, cheese, and a pinch of salt, and beat until creamy and smooth. Cover and set aside to let the batter rest for at least 1 hour.

2. Meanwhile, bring a large pot of salted water to a boil over high heat. Put the whole head of cauliflower into the pot and cook for 5 to 6 minutes. It should remain firm. Separate the cauliflower into florets and put in colander set over a bowl to drain well.

3. When ready to cook, pour oil into a wide, heavy medium pot to a depth of 2 inches and heat over medium-high heat until a deep-fry or candy thermometer inserted in the oil reads 350°F. Working in batches, spear a floret with a fork and dip into the batter to coat all over. Using a second fork, gently pry the cauliflower

into the oil. Fry until golden brown. Using a slotted spoon, transfer the cauli-flower to paper towels to drain. Season with salt immediately while still hot. Be sure to allow oil to return to 350°F between batches. Serve hot.

Note: Visit www.gethsemanifarms.org to purchase Gethsemani cheese.

Anyone who has ever eaten a delicious helping of spanakopita in a good Greek diner knows that the flavors of spinach and cheese make a winning combination. Here they come together in a recipe for crêpes that is as delicious as it is healthy. It has been adapted from Brother Victor-Antoine d'Avila-Latourrette's book From a Monastery Kitchen: The Classic Natural Foods Cookbook.

CRÊPES

    2 eggs

    1 cup whole milk

    1 cup all-purpose flour

    1 tablespoon canola or vegetable oil or unsalted butter, melted

FILLING

    3 tablespoons unsalted butter

    1 onion, chopped

    2 cloves garlic, minced

    8 ounces frozen spinach, thawed, drained, and chopped

    4 eggs, hard-cooked and chopped

    1 cup (about 2½ ounces) coarsely grated Gethsemani cheese (see Note) or other
        Trappist-style cheese

CREAM SAUCE

    3 tablespoons all-purpose flour

    1½ cups whole milk

    3 tablespoons unsalted butter

    Nutmeg

    Salt and freshly ground black pepper

1. For the crêpes: Beat the eggs and milk thoroughly in a large bowl, then beat in the flour. Strain through a fine-mesh strainer set over a bowl to remove lumps. Let the batter rest, covered, in the refrigerator for 1 hour.

2. Heat a 7-inch crêpe pan or 8-inch nonstick skillet over medium heat until hot, then very lightly brush with oil or melted butter. Give the batter a quick stir, then pour in just enough batter to lightly coat the bottom of the pan (about 2 tablespoons), tilting and rotating the pan as you pour to evenly distribute the batter. Cook one side until light golden, about 1½ minutes, then loosen the edges and flip using a spatula. Cook the other side for another minute. Transfer the crêpes to a sheet pan as they are done, overlapping the crêpes slightly. Continue making crêpes, brushing the pan with butter as necessary, until you use up all the batter. You should have about 12 crêpes.

3. For the filling: Melt the butter in a nonreactive large pan over medium heat. Add the onions and sweat until softened but not browned, 6 to 8 minutes, then add the garlic and cook for 1 minute. Add the spinach and toss to mix well. Transfer the mixture to a wide, shallow bowl, add the eggs, and cool slightly. Stir in the cheese and set aside.

4. For the sauce: Dissolve the flour in ½ cup of the milk. Melt the butter in a medium skillet over medium heat. When it begins foaming, add the milk mixture, whisking constantly. Add the remaining milk and season with nutmeg and salt

and pepper to taste. Stir until the sauce comes to a simmer, then lower the heat and continue stirring until the sauce thickens and is smooth, about 15 minutes.

5. Preheat the oven to 450°F. Place 2 to 3 tablespoons of the filling in a line down the center of each crêpe, roll up snugly, and arrange in a 9 × 13-inch baking dish. Spread the sauce over the crêpes and bake until the sauce is bubbling and browned in spots, about 15 minutes. Let cool slightly before serving.

Note: Visit www.gethsemanifarms.org to purchase Gethsemani cheese.

SWEET TEMPTATIONS

Eat honey, my son, for it is good.

—PROVERBS 24:13

Look, there's no metaphysics on earth like chocolates.
—FERNANDO PESSOA, PORTUGUESE POET (1888–1935)

oney was the only available sweetener in the Middle Ages. Cooks used it to make a heavy spice cake that would last for days (also known as *pain d'épices* in France, where abbeys such as Oelenberg in Alsace and La Joie-Notre-Dame in Brittany still make it). Mead was a popular fermented drink in the Middle Ages that was made with honey and water; it is still made by commercial producers but is no longer made by monasteries.

Sugar is a relatively new invention, but it has been put to good use by monks and nuns. In the United States the nuns at Mississippi Abbey in Iowa and Mount Saint Mary's in Massachusetts are expert candymakers, while Dominican nuns at the Monastery of the Angels just outside Hollywood make handmade candy that is sold only in the gift shop. In Belgium, sugar and butter come together in the sublime cookies made by nuns at the Abbey of Clairefontaine (try the ones shaped like ladyfingers and layered with chocolate).

Arab culture influenced the cuisine of southern Europe for hundreds of years, including sweets. Monasteries in southern Spain and Italy invented sweets that used traditional Middle Eastern ingredients such as almonds, pistachios, and honey. Only two Italian monasteries still make their own food products for sale (wine and jam); others license their products to commercial vendors.

Most of the Spanish nuns who still make sweets can be found in and around Seville, while nuns at the Monastery of Santo Domingo el Antiguo in Toledo continue to make marzipan. Spanish nuns are cloistered in a stricter sense than nuns in the United States and the rest of Europe, and few offer retreats (one exception is the nuns of Santa María del Socorro, who accept guests for short stays and make a variety of delightful sweets, including their irresistible anise-flavored *pestiños*). Spanish monasteries also have a quirky tradition of selling sweets through turnstiles. Put your money on the turnstile and it comes back with your order—this is the closest a visitor will get to meeting many of the Spanish nuns who make food.

Eggs and especially egg yolks played an important role in sweets made by nuns in Spain and Portugal, where they were used in treats that were sold to raise money for the poor. *Yemas* are a typical Spanish sweet made with egg yolks; the most famous are *yemas de Ávila*, named after the town where Saint Teresa lived. In Portugal, sweets made at monasteries such as the sixteenth-century Convento da Graça in the Algarve (now a hotel, a fate suffered all too often by former monasteries) carried inventive names like mother-in-law's eyes (*olhos de sogra*), sighs (*suspiros*), nuns' tummies (*barrigas de freiras*), and bacon from heaven (*toucinho do céu*); the last is a rich custard originally made with lard bacon. There are no monasteries in Portugal that still make edible sweets, although the Monastery of Singeverga makes a sweet liqueur.

German monasteries were once famous for their gingerbread, as was the Monastery of Einsiedeln in Switzerland, which no longer makes gingerbread but remains a major shrine that attracts more than 100,000 pilgrims each year (and which is the mother-house of Saint Meinrad in Indiana). Monasteries often kept bees as a source of candle wax and used their honey to make gingerbread and mead. Secular bakers in Nuremberg put gingerbread on the culinary map in a big way with their imaginative variations on the spicy cookie, including *Honigkuchen, Pfefferkuchen, Lebkuchen, Pfefferzelten, Leb-zelten,* and *Pfeffernüsse.* Europe even had professional gingerbread guilds and wood carv-ers competing to make the most elaborate gingerbread molds.

Hundreds of monasteries still make food in France (see www.monastic-euro.org for a comprehensive list). The Benedictine Abbey of Saint Guénolé in Brittany makes a tra-ditional Gallic treat, *pâtes de fruits,* with fruit from its own orchards; other good sources for these fruity chews are the Abbaye Notre-Dame de Tournay in the Midi-Pyrénées and the Monastery of Notre-Dame de Protection in Lower Normandy, which coats its *pâtes de fruits* in chocolate. If you prefer almonds, try the celestially inspired Rocaman-dines from the Monastère de la Paix-Dieu in Languedoc-Roussillon, where the nuns take balls of almond paste, cover them in chocolate, and roll them in roasted almonds from Provence.

The United Kingdom is known for its delicious scones and hard candy. If you like shortbread, you will say a prayer when you taste the cookies made by the monks of Caldey Island Monastery off the coast of Wales (they ship to the United States). The monastery can be reached only by boat and is not accessible year-round; however, it is a wonderful day trip in the tourist season.

OUR LADY OF CONSOLATION PRIORY

NEAR AMITY, OREGON

One half expects to be followed around by a hungry unicorn at this priory, where the lush grass is a particularly enticing shade of emerald green. Alas, there have been no sightings of the fabled beast here, but the place is still enchanting. At Easter the grounds are fairly dripping with flowers—daffodils nod gently in the breeze, cherry blossoms dangle like earrings hung from leafy lobes, and hyacinths scent the air. A statue of Mary watches over a menagerie of birds and beasts (including several rescued cats) who cavort on the lawn. It feels as though one has entered the magical world of a medieval tapestry, like the ones at the Cloisters in New York or the Musée de Cluny (Musée National du

Moyen Age) in Paris, and been given the chance to frolic among elegant maidens, fanciful creatures, and carpets of flowers.

This priory appears small on a geographical map, but its spiritual footprint is grand. Our Lady of Consolation was founded in 1976 by Brother Benedict Kirby and belongs to the Order of Our Most Holy Savior; the order was founded by Saint Bridget of Sweden in 1370 and follows the Rule of Saint Augustine. The monks endured years of poverty and other hardships before settling in the Yamhill Valley, which is as famous for its superb wines as it is for the monks' fudge and truffles.

A visitor may be surprised to find that this petite priory is the source of truffles whose fame has spread far and wide, thanks to mentions on *ABC Nightly News*, CNN, and even *Jeopardy!* The monks also make silky-smooth fudge. Try the chocolate fudge (with or without nuts) or the pecan-praline fudge, which is made with brown sugar and is melt-in-your-mouth good. Seasonal flavors include a dense Chocolate Cherry Nut Fudge, which is as much fun to chew as it is delicious.

The priory's truffles are as unpretentious as are the monks who make them. Visitors won't find gold leaf or flavors like sushi here, but they will find truffles that are as big as a golf ball and come in delicious flavors like raspberry, butter rum, and dark chocolate. The charming truffle box shows the monks making candy in old-fashioned copper kettles.

In an unusual twist of fate, Oregon is now home to the only Brigittine monks in the world. The Brigittine Order thrived in the Middle Ages, but religious persecution and the Reformation dealt it a double blow; by the end of the nineteenth century there were no Brigittine monks left (although the nuns fared somewhat better). The monks at Our Lady of Consolation have revived the spirit and traditions of the order, right down to their distinctive habits, which were sewn by Brigittine nuns in Mexico and, according to Saint Bridget's instructions, are gray like the ashes that Jews and Christians once wore as a symbol of penitence.

A lovely bronze figure of Mary, sculpted by a local artist, keeps watch over guests on retreat. She is serenaded by a robust chorus of tree frogs by night and a symphony of birds by day; in fact, there are so many birds here that it seems as though the Ark had just disembarked. In medieval Europe, illiterate peasants would "read" the stained-glass windows that recounted biblical scenes in rich reds, golds, greens, and especially blue, a color that was often associated with Mary. One can't help but think of her here, where everything from the grape hyacinths and rain-dark clouds to the distant Coast Range Mountains seems saturated with a particularly majestic shade of blue.

The sense one has that this priory is a little patch of Eden is reinforced by the abundant flowers. The path that leads to the guesthouse is lined with heirloom roses, daffodils, hyacinths, primrose, tulips, and camellias. In Saint Bridget's day, every aspect of a Christian's life was filled with symbolic meaning, including flowers and herbs; a contemporary gardener who plants lady's mantle (*Alchemilla vulgaris*) may not realize that this plant, like so many others, once made people think of Mary. Other flowers that are associated with Mary to this day are the Madonna lily (a favorite with painters of the Annunciation) and the rose.

We often associate the Middle Ages with disease and hardship, but they were also a time when a simple flower could turn one's thoughts toward God, and Saint Bridget planted the seeds of an order that would bear fruit in Oregon centuries later. She once had a vision in which she took refuge under Mary's cloak, where she felt enveloped by humility. One can contemplate the examples of Bridget and Mary—how they acted with humility and listened to God's will with open hearts—while strolling in the gardens at the Cloisters or viewing the ethereal Unicorn tapestries in Paris. One can also stay home and munch on fudge while planting lady's mantle and contemplating a piece of advice that Mary gave to Bridget: Flee the inconstancy of the world, which is only a false vision and a quickly fading flower.

The Brigittine monks made cake, zucchini bread, and pumpkin bread before they got into the candy business. However, the baked goods didn't generate enough income to sustain the priory in its early years. Meanwhile, one of the monks began experimenting with different fudge recipes, and the other monks were happy to act as taste-testers. The monks finally developed a recipe they all liked and began to make fudge instead of baked goods. The truffles, which were added later, quickly became best-sellers.

The monks got some expert advice in their early years from an anonymous candy technician who used to work for a famous candy company. He was also the source of their original truffle recipe, but the monks are quick to point out that they have since refined the recipe to make it their own.

The monks sell almost exclusively to customers in the United States. They say their delicious fudge is so dense that overseas customers would end up paying more for shipping than for the fudge itself!

FOOD PRODUCTS: Fudge, truffles

GUESTHOUSE: Yes, M/F

WEBSITE: www.brigittine.org

ORDER: Phone, fax, e-mail, or write

E-MAIL: fudge@brigittine.org

PHONE: 503-835-8080

FAX: 503-835-9662

GUESTHOUSE E-MAIL: monks@brigittine.org (put "Guest" in the subject line)

Our Lady of Consolation Priory

The Brigittine Monks

23300 Walker Lane

Amity, OR 97101

MOUNT SAINT MARY'S ABBEY

NEAR WRENTHAM, MASSACHUSETTS

Tourists in New England expect to see lobsters. The crustaceans appear on menus, license plates, and store shingles. There are lobster candies, cookie cutters, and key chains. Of course, real New Englanders know to go down to the dock for live lobsters, fresh from the trap. What neither tourists nor natives expect to see here is a creature who looks like he was headed for the Inca ruins of Peru but ended up at an abbey closer to Boston: a llama named Oblio. Llamas are sometimes called "camels of the clouds" for their ability to haul mountain loads, yet Oblio looks like he's dressed for a dinner party in a snowy white tux with black tails. Visitors who buy the abbey's wool blankets can thank Oblio for protecting the sheep from coyotes.

In addition to a llama, this monastery is home to some of New England's best candy. Mount Saint Mary's Abbey was founded in 1949 by nuns from Saint Mary's Abbey in

Glencairn, Ireland; it was the first American monastery founded by Cistercian nuns. The abbey church is austere in a way that reflects Trappist traditions; its stark white walls and low ceiling make the space feel humble and intimate. However, one's eye is drawn to a detail that is as unexpected here as a llama in Massachusetts: the Salve Regina window, which was made for the nuns by a monk from Holy Spirit Monastery in Georgia. It is so colorful that it looks as though the glass had been fused with celestial fire. The nuns agree that it's unusual, but like the way its light captures the tone of each prayer throughout the day.

Candy lovers in New England fondly remember Crand's Candy Castle in Enfield, Connecticut. Its owner was a Greek immigrant named John Crand who taught the nuns how to make candy. He insisted on using the best ingredients regardless of cost, and that's the way the nuns make candy to this day. One can taste the difference from bags of store-bought candy at the first bite of the monastery's Butter Nut Munch, a delicious

almond-butter candy that is coated with chocolate and hazelnuts. The nuns' artisanal chocolates are also divine (especially the dark chocolate with almonds), and their Maple Walnut Penuche (pronounced peh-*noo*-chee) is an old New England favorite made with brown sugar and cream.

It would take a saint's level of restraint to order only one kind of candy from Mount Saint Mary's, so try sharing it with others in order to avoid gluttony. The nuns make sharing easy, thanks to their clever candy samplers: the Dark Chocolate Trappistine Assortment comes with a hand-decorated bar of dark chocolate that is as pretty as it is delicious, while the Trappistine Treasure Deluxe combines an assortment of the nuns' finest candies with jars of preserves from Saint Joseph's Abbey (the monks at Saint Joseph's originally introduced the nuns to John Crand).

The nuns also offer a candy sampler that includes a bottle of Mepkin Abbey's Drizzzle, a tart-and-sweet condiment that can be a tasty topping for ice cream and waffles (one of Mepkin Abbey's monks is an expert baker, whose book *Baking with Brother Boniface: Recipes from the Kitchen of Mepkin Abbey* is available at www.mepkinabbey.org). But the best sampler of all may be the one that combines Butter Nut Munch with jars of honey from Redwoods Abbey in California (www.redwoodsabbey.org)—what gift could be sweeter than that! Just beware—this candy is good enough to convert one's casual candy habit into a candy obsession.

Conversion hangs in the air like incense at Wrentham. It's a place where everything expresses the potential to be transformed: light converts stained glass into molten color, cold weather changes autumn leaves to gold and red, and chocolate becomes a heavenly treat. Sometimes the place transforms people. A nun who was asked by a guest how she found her vocation to a contemplative life said she came to Mount Saint Mary's three times, prayed each time to ask if she should stay, and received three affirmative answers. It's nice to think that a heart that is open to conversion may find it here.

Guests on retreat can ponder other examples of people who answered a call to a vocation. When Thomas Merton converted to Catholicism and became a Trappist monk, he left behind an agnostic life in New York; *The Seven Storey Mountain* tells the story of his conversion. Saint Francis was a wealthy young nobleman when he had a conversion of heart and exchanged worldly riches for a different kind of treasure—and Helen Keller, who lived in Wrentham, let nothing stand in the way of her vocation to communicate with the world.

All hearts, religious or secular, should strive to be converted toward peace. Have some Butter Nut Munch or chocolate with almonds, and take a few deep breaths. Listen to Giovanni Battista Pergolesi's arrangement for the Salve Regina prayer (and consider that he wrote it on his deathbed at the tender age of twenty-six) and think about the lovely window at Mount Saint Mary's. Then tip your hat to Wrentham's Irish roots and spend a few moments contemplating this simple Scots Gaelic prayer: "Peace between neighbors, Peace between kindred, Peace between lovers . . . Peace between person and person, Peace between wife and husband, Peace between woman and children, The peace of Christ above all peace."

When Mount Saint Mary's was founded, the nuns made caramels using a recipe from a candymaker who was a friend of the monastery. They no longer make caramels, but they make a mouthwatering variety of other candy, including brown sugar fudge and chocolate.

The nuns also sell blankets that are made with wool from their own sheep. Until recently the monastery owned cattle and the nuns milked cows (the abbey was founded by nuns from Ireland, where some monasteries are still farming).

FOOD PRODUCTS: Butter Nut Munch, chocolates, fudge, penuche, candy
combos

GUESTHOUSE: Yes, M/F

WEBSITE: http://abbey.msmabbey.org

CANDY WEBSITE: www.TrappistineCandy.com

ORDER: E-mail, phone, or write

E-MAIL: orders@trappistinecandy.com

PHONE: 866-549-8929 (toll-free)

GUESTHOUSE PHONE: 508-528-1282

    Mount Saint Mary's Abbey

    Trappistine Quality Candy

    300 Arnold Street

    Wrentham, MA 02093

Rick Bayless is one of those chefs who clearly has a vocation. For the rest of us—whose calling is to raise a family or to be a good friend to others—this is the perfect recipe to make and share, and the combination of pecans and chocolate could make an angel swoon. Chef Bayless kindly provided this recipe, which has been adapted from his book Rick Bayless's Mexican Kitchen: Capturing the Vibrant Flavors of a World-Class Cuisine, *written with Deann Groen Bayless and Jeanmarie Brownson.*

CRUST

   1½ cups all-purpose flour

   6 tablespoons chilled unsalted butter, cut into ½-inch bits

   3 tablespoons vegetable shortening or rich-tasting lard, chilled and cut into
       ½-inch bits

   ¾ teaspoon sugar

   ¼ teaspoon salt

   1 egg yolk, beaten slightly

FILLING

   2 cups pecan halves (make sure they're fresh and richly flavorful)

   6 ounces semisweet or Mount Saint Mary's bittersweet chocolate (see Note)

   3 tablespoons all-purpose flour

   ¾ cup room-temperature unsalted butter

   1 cup firmly packed dark brown sugar

   5 large eggs, at room temperature

   ¾ cup light corn syrup

   ¼ cup molasses

   1½ tablespoons Kahlúa or brandy

2¼ teaspoons vanilla extract

½ teaspoon salt

2 cups sweetened whipped cream flavored with Kahlúa for serving

1. For the crust: Combine the flour, butter, and shortening (or lard) into a bowl or food processor fitted with the metal blade. Quickly work the fats into the flour with a pastry blender or pulse the food processor until the flour looks a little damp (not powdery) but tiny bits of fat are still visible. If using the food processor, transfer the mixture to a bowl.

2. Mix together the sugar, salt, and 3 tablespoons of ice water in a small bowl. Using a fork, little by little work the ice-water mixture into the flour mixture. The dough will be in rough, rather stiff clumps; if there is unincorporated flour in the bottom of the bowl, sprinkle in a little more ice water and use the fork to work it together. Press the dough together into a flat disk, wrap in plastic, and refrigerate at least 1 hour.

3. On a lightly floured surface, roll the dough into a 12-inch circle. Transfer to a deep 10-inch glass pie pan (I find it easiest to roll the dough onto a rolling pin, then unroll it onto the pie pan). Decoratively crimp the edge and trim excess dough. Refrigerate for 30 minutes.

4. Prebake the crust: Preheat the oven to 400°F. Lightly oil a 15-inch piece of foil and lay it oiled-side down into the crust (heavy-duty foil is too stiff to work here); press down to line the crust snugly. Fill with beans or pie weights and bake for about 15 minutes, until beginning to brown around the edges. Reduce the oven temperature to 350°F. Carefully remove the beans or weights and foil, return the crust to the oven, and bake for 8 to 10 minutes, until it no longer looks moist. (If it bubbles at this point, gently press it down with the back of a spoon.) Leave the oven on. Brush the beaten egg yolk over the crust, then let cool completely.

5. Prepare the nuts and chocolate: While the crust is cooling, spread the pecans on a baking sheet and toast in the oven until fragrant, about 10 minutes. Cool, then break into small pieces and transfer to a large bowl. Chop the chocolate into rough, ½-inch pieces and add to the bowl, along with the flour. Stir until everything is well coated.

6. For the filling: In a food processor (or in the large bowl of an electric mixer), cream the butter and brown sugar until light and fluffy, about 3 minutes in the food processor, 5 minutes in the mixer. With the machine still running, add the eggs, one at a time, letting each be completely incorporated before adding the next. Beat in the corn syrup, molasses, Kahlúa or brandy, vanilla, and salt.

7. Pour the filling over the chocolate and pecans and stir well to combine. Pour the mixture into the prebaked pie shell, set onto the lower shelf of the oven, and bake until a knife inserted into the center comes out clean, about 1 hour. Cool on a wire rack. Serve slices of the pie at room temperature or slightly warm, topped with a dollop of Kahlúa-spiked sweetened whipped cream.

Advance Preparation—The pie can be made several days ahead, wrapped in plastic and refrigerated. It freezes well. Because the pie is easiest to cut when cold, I suggest making it ahead, refrigerating it, cutting it, then warming just before serving.

Variations and Improvisations—Other nuts can be substituted for the pecans. Honey can replace the molasses for a lighter flavor. If you like the crystalline crunch of Mexican chocolate, reduce the semisweet chocolate to 5 ounces and sprinkle the pie with ⅓ cup rather finely chopped Mexican chocolate before baking.

Note: Visit www.abbey.msmabbey.org to purchase Mount Saint Mary's chocolate.

OUR LADY OF THE MISSISSIPPI ABBEY

NEAR DUBUQUE, IOWA

Two New Yorkers happened to share a recent flight over Iowa. One had just been to an abbey, where she spent the time in silence with only birds and the wind in the trees for companions. It was very peaceful. The other was on his way to a meeting, armed with a laptop, cell phone, headphones, and handheld device. He could not sit still. The guest who had just left the abbey remembered what it was like to be on call twenty-four hours a day—it wasn't peaceful. She turned to her seatmate and offered him a caramel made by the nuns at the abbey, hoping that he might get a taste of inner peace simply by association, but he was too busy to accept.

If life seems too busy to make time for this abbey's caramels, it might be a good idea to reconsider priorities. These just might be the best caramels you will ever taste. Mississippi Abbey was founded in 1964 by nuns from Mount Saint Mary's Abbey in Massachusetts and belongs to the Order of Cistercians of the Strict Observance (also known as Trappists). The original recipe for Trappistine Creamy Caramels came from the abbey's motherhouse, where the nuns are also expert candy makers.

All caramel lovers have experienced heartache in pursuit of the object of their desire. Caramels can be something of a tease, promising sweet riches with their tawny glow and shiny wrapper but delivering a spiteful leaden lump to the taste buds. Next to those kinds of caramels, Trappistine Creamy Caramels are a buttery epiphany. They are made with fresh butter and cream from local farms, which helps give them a silky-smooth texture that is sublime. The nuns make caramels in vanilla and chocolate flavors and vanilla caramels covered in light or dark chocolate, as well as mints for the holiday season. Caramel lovers face but one dilemma: Which flavor to sample first? Now, that may call for a prayer.

The abbey's candy factory offers no visible or olfactory clues about the culinary transformation that takes place inside. It is a one-story brusque brick building with few windows. Cross the threshold, however, and candy lovers may think they have stepped into a scene from *Charlie and the Chocolate Factory*. Vanilla and chocolate aromas waft through the air; machines whirl, clank

and whine; gas burners roar to life; and copper kettles bubble with golden caramel.

Caramels endure a kind of candy boot camp before making their retail debut. They are beaten in an industrial mixer, chilled on cooling tables, sliced, diced, and finally wrapped in a cellophane girdle to maintain their figure and freshness. (The nuns weed out caramels that they say are "geometrically challenged" and use them to fill the candy jars in the guesthouse.) Mississippi Abbey caramels have been lauded by *U.S. News & World Report* and the Food Network, and a team pastor used to give them to the New York Yankees for the holidays.

A visit to this abbey leads one to begin to think about the nature of work. The nuns work hard. (Just try putting those little chocolate curlicues on top of the chocolate-covered caramels when they are speeding by—it's reminiscent of the oft-cited *I Love Lucy* episode where she can't keep up with the candy conveyor belt!) They also work in silence. Nevertheless, there is a sense of camaraderie here that is different from a typical office. The nuns don't live to work, they live to pray.

If only a stressed-out employee like the one on the flight over Iowa could look up from his laptop for a moment, he might glimpse Mississippi Abbey's dappled forests and rustic pastures bathed in an effervescent light worthy of Monet. He could see the majestic river wind its way darkly at the foot of a wooded valley, and watch the wind carve a path through the trees.

It's no wonder that an Iowa grandmother who likes to visit the abbey says she feels like she is on hallowed ground. The place is beautiful right down to the smallest detail, like the cast-iron horse's head that adorns the abbey well, and the grounds convey a profound sense of peace. Life in the monastery has a steady pace that is comforting rather than constraining. The nuns follow Saint Benedict's instruction to place prayer and the Divine Office above all else. They even take a prayer break in the middle of their work shift, which just might explain why these caramels taste heavenly!

When Mount Saint Mary's Abbey sent thirteen nuns to Iowa in 1964 to found Our Lady of the Mississippi, the nuns brought along a recipe for making caramels. Over the years Mississippi has continued to specialize in caramels, while Mount Saint Mary's has specialized in other kinds of candy.

Like other abbeys, the nuns once farmed for a living. They used to raise crops including soy, corn, oats, and alfalfa and even grew Christmas trees. They also raised sheep for wool. They now rent their pastures to neighboring farmers and have hired a professional forester to manage their woodlands.

FOOD PRODUCTS: Caramels, caramel sauce, mints, truffles (truffles made for, but not by, the nuns)

GUESTHOUSE: Yes, M/F

WEBSITE: www.mississippiabbey.org

CANDY WEBSITE: www.trappistine.com

ORDER: E-mail, phone, or write

E-MAIL: questions@monasterycandy.com

PHONE: 866-556-3400 (toll-free)

GUESTHOUSE CONTACT: Use the online form at the abbey's website.

Our Lady of the Mississippi Abbey

Trappistine Creamy Caramels

8318 Abbey Hill Lane

Dubuque, IA 52003

Brother Victor's Pear Clafoutis

(Pears Baked in Custard with Caramels)   *Makes one 9 × 13 clafoutis, 6 to 12 servings*

Clafoutis is a classic French dessert with a consistency somewhere between a custard and a sponge cake; it is traditionally made with fresh cherries. This dessert is as popular with adults as it is with children, and some fans of clafoutis will go to great lengths to seek out their favorite version (check out Bittersweet Pastry Shop's clafoutis the next time you're in Chicago). Brother Victor-Antoine d'Avila-Latourrette generously shared this recipe so that clafoutis lovers everywhere can make it at home.

Unsalted butter for the baking dish

6 small ripe Bosc pears (see Notes)

3 eggs

½ cup granulated sugar

2 teaspoons cornstarch

1½ cups whole milk

2 tablespoons cognac or pear brandy

1 teaspoon vanilla extract

Pinch of freshly grated nutmeg

12 to 14 individual Mississippi Abbey Trappistine vanilla caramels (see Notes),
     or other caramels of your choice, unwrapped

1. Preheat the oven to 350°F. Generously butter a large 9 × 13-inch baking dish and set aside. Peel, halve, and core the pears and set aside.

2. In a medium bowl, whisk together the eggs, sugar, and cornstarch. Add the milk, cognac, and vanilla and mix until well combined. Pour a thin layer, about 1 cup, of the custard into the baking dish, tilting the pan to spread it evenly over

the bottom of the pan. Bake in the center of the oven until the custard thickens and sets, about 5 minutes. Remove the pan from the oven and carefully arrange the pears cut side down over the set custard. Pour the rest of the custard over the fruit and sprinkle the nutmeg lightly over the top. Arrange the caramels about 2 inches apart on the top of the clafoutis. Return to the oven and bake until the custard is firm and starts to brown around the edges a bit, 40 to 45 minutes.

3. Remove the clafoutis from the oven and serve warm.

Notes: Brother Victor says you can experiment with other kinds of fruit, but you may need to adjust the amount of sugar.

Visit www.trappistine.com to purchase Mississippi Abbey caramels.

It helps to know that Alain Coumont is Belgian. Belgium is a country where it is very hard to eat anything but extraordinary food, from simple yet delicious mussels and fries to hearty soups and sophisticated ales. Coumont was one of the first chefs to introduce world-class bread and pastries to New York when he opened Le Pain Quotidien. Brownie lovers have beaten a path to his door ever since; served with ice cream and the nuns' caramel sauce, these brownies are a true taste of heaven.

8 ounces bittersweet chocolate, roughly chopped

8 ounces (2 sticks) unsalted butter, cut into small pieces

3 tablespoons pastry flour or 2 tablespoons cake flour plus 1 tablespoon all-
     purpose flour

1 cup plus 1½ tablespoons superfine sugar

4 large eggs plus 1 egg yolk, beaten

Walnut halves (optional)

Vanilla ice cream or lightly sweetened whipped cream

Mississippi Abbey Trappistine Creamy Caramel Sauce (see Note)

1. In a double boiler or a metal bowl set over a saucepan of barely simmering water, melt the chocolate and butter together, stirring occasionally, until smooth. Transfer the chocolate mixture to a large bowl. Let cool slightly. Meanwhile, sift the flour into the sugar and stir to combine. Whisk into the eggs. Fold the egg mixture into the chocolate mixture with a spatula. Set aside and let rest for 30 minutes.

2. Preheat the oven to 275°F. Stir the walnuts into the batter, if using. Divide

the batter among 12 to 15 paper-lined muffin tin holes and bake in the center of the oven until the edges are firm and the tops have formed a thin wrinkled crust, about 40 minutes. Cool the brownies in the tins on a rack.

3. Serve slightly warm with a scoop of vanilla ice cream or whipped cream and drizzle with caramel sauce. As the butter and chocolate content of these brownies is very high, they keep perfectly for a week if stored in a metal tin at room temperature, or for up to 2 months in the freezer in an air-tight bag.

Note: Visit www.trappistine.com to order Mississippi Abbey Trappistine Creamy Caramel Sauce.

OUR LADY OF BONNEVAL ABBEY

NEAR ESPALION IN AVEYRON, FRANCE

It doesn't take long for a visitor to notice there's something different about these woods: one minute they're silent, and the next it's practically raining chestnuts. They hit the ground with a startling syncopated rhythm that sounds as if Emeril were nearby—*bam, bam . . . bam!* Chestnuts are nicknamed "the poor man's potato," and the number of ways they can be used in soups, stews, desserts, and other recipes is limited only by a cook's imagination. One wishes Emeril *were* here to whip up a chestnut purée or a pot of *aligot*—a local dish of mashed potatoes thickened with Cantal cheese. However, food lovers don't need a celebrity chef to eat well in Aveyron; it's easy to find great food here, including Roquefort cheese, Marcillac wines, and chocolates from Bonneval.

Abbaye Notre-Dame de Bonneval was founded in 1147 and belongs to the Order of Cistercians of the Strict Observance, also known as Trappists; it was founded not long after Cîteaux. Bonneval is on a mountain so steep that the monks had to terrace the land just to build here; the American monk Thomas Merton once wrote that Bonneval is a perfect example of Cistercian foolishness, because one would have to be foolish to build here in the first place! The abbey feels like a castle and a country estate all rolled up in one, and its unusual floor plan requires a visitor to walk outside the abbey walls and hike up a daunting hill to reach the church. The effort is worthwhile: the path takes one past forbidding lookout towers, ancient woods, and exuberant flowers.

You can't help but notice Bonneval's massive fortified walls. They are extremely thick and high, but not thick or high enough to keep out the English during the Hundred Years' War when the abbey was repeatedly attacked. In 1791 the French accomplished what the English could not; they pillaged the abbey and evicted the monks. Cistercian nuns arrived in 1875 to reclaim Bonneval but faced a formidable task. The abbey church lay in ruins with nothing but open sky for a roof (there's an old photo of Bonneval that shows the nuns clearing the rubble with a wheelbarrow, one stone at a time). The nuns here will convince any doubting Thomas that all things are possible with God. Not only did they construct a new church—hauntingly beautiful in its austerity—but they also built a chocolate factory and a hydroelectric power generator to run it. Theirs is now the sole abbey in France that makes chocolate from scratch, sourcing the best cocoa powder from top producers.

One is never quite sure if the nuns or Mother Nature has the upper hand at Bonneval. Ancient stone walls in the woods ooze thick carpets of moss, birds boisterously rule the treetops, and giant slugs with gourmand tastes claim the forest floor, where they slurp up the rains and dine on girolle mushrooms; a hiker will notice that there seems to be an evolutionary struggle going on between the man-made fences that enclose the mountain pastures and hungry sheep who think the grass looks greener on the other side (the slopes here are too steep for cows). Don't bring your big-city uptight attitude here because it will not serve you well. Instead, do as the nuns do: set your priorities, don't sweat the small stuff—and eat chocolate.

This shouldn't be hard to do. The nuns make chocolates filled with liqueur (in rum, pear, and triple orange flavors), praline-filled chocolates, cream-filled chocolates, and chocolate bars in dark, milk, and hazelnut flavors; there's even a chocolate bar that is

 flavored with coffee from the Cistercian Monastery of Koutaba in Cameroon. Best of all, the heady scent of rich hot cocoa greets guests at breakfast every morning and forms a lingering olfactory memory that could give Proust's madeleines a run for their money. Chocoholics can see the chocolate-making process step by step (with descriptions in French) on the abbey's website.

A charming Romanesque Madonna is enthroned with her child above the abbey's entrance gate, where she calmly watches over the nuns, guests on retreat, and visitors who come to buy chocolates and gather chestnuts. She's been here since the twelfth century, and she miraculously survived the French Revolution unscathed. Her smile is so gentle that it makes one smile in turn; one of the nuns thinks the sculptor modeled her after his own wife and baby, since she clasps the infant Jesus to her breast just as a real mother would a newborn. Whatever the source of the artist's inspiration, it's nice to think that as long as Our Lady of Bonneval remains safe then so will the abbey.

The nuns are always open to expanding their product line, but quite frankly they could use some extra help. One can't help but wonder why more women don't come to stay for good in a place as peaceful and beautiful as this, so here's a quick review of the benefits: The nuns are friendly, the Mother Abbess is kind, this is the closest one will ever get to living in a castle, and there is plenty of chocolate to eat. There's even a young nun here who speaks perfect English (and who previously worked as a computer chip designer), so this is the perfect place to explore a vocation.

Bonneval especially feels like a lost paradise right before Lauds, when the mountains wear the pale pink sky like a cloak with a crescent moon for its clasp. Maybe the Cistercians who chose this site for an abbey were crazy—crazy like a fox. Highways and suburbs will never plague this place because the mountains are too steep; a guest who was late for church was recently reminded just how steep they are when she tried to run uphill and was almost forced to a crawl (maybe the nuns should call it Merton's Hill). It's better not to run here, so leave plenty of time to get to church and remember to say a prayer that Aveyron will always be home to the nuns who make divine chocolate.

FOOD PRODUCTS: Chocolates

GUESTHOUSE: Yes, M/F

WEBSITE: www.abbaye-bonneval.com

ORDER: E-mail or phone

E-MAIL: info@abbaye-bonneval.com

NOTE: For international calls, first dial 011 from the United States or 00 from Europe, then 33 for France, followed by the local phone number listed below; if the local number begins with a zero, drop it when dialing from abroad.

PHONE: (0)5 65 44 01 22

GUESTHOUSE E-MAIL: hotellerie@abbaye-bonneval.com

GUESTHOUSE PHONE: (0)5 65 44 48 83

Bonneval Abbey

F-12500 Le Cayrol

France

Chocolate Chestnut Torte with Cognac Mousse

Makes one 3-layer 8-inch cake (8 servings)

If you want to make this amazing torte with Bonneval chocolate, you just might have to go to France, since American distributors for the abbey's chocolate are still scarce. Of course, any excuse to visit Bonneval is a good excuse! Otherwise, try using Lindt or Ghirardelli bittersweet chocolate. This recipe has been adapted from www.epicurious .com and Gourmet magazine (December 2002).

GANACHE FILLING AND FROSTING

2 cups heavy cream

½ stick (¼ cup) unsalted butter

16 ounces Bonneval bittersweet chocolate (see Notes) or other fine bittersweet chocolate, finely chopped

6 marrons glacés (candied chestnuts; see Notes), finely chopped

CAKE LAYERS

9 ounces bottled whole shelled roasted chestnuts (1½ cups)

2 cups cake flour (not self-rising)

1½ teaspoons baking soda

½ teaspoon salt

2 sticks (1 cup) unsalted butter, softened

1½ cups packed light brown sugar

4 large eggs

1 teaspoon vanilla extract

¾ cup sour cream

COGNAC MOUSSE

¾ stick (6 tablespoons) unsalted butter, cut into pieces

8 ounces Bonneval bittersweet chocolate or other fine bittersweet chocolate

    (not unsweetened), finely chopped

5 tablespoons cognac

¾ cup chilled heavy cream

2 large egg whites

¼ cup granulated sugar

SPECIAL EQUIPMENT: 3 (8-inch) round cake pans; an 8-inch round of cardboard,

    covered with foil if not wax-coated

1. For the ganache: Bring the cream and butter to a simmer in a 3- to 4-quart heavy saucepan, then reduce the heat to low. Whisk in the chocolate until smooth and remove from the heat. Transfer the ganache to a bowl and chill, covered, stirring every 30 minutes, until thickened but spreadable, about 2 hours. (If the ganache becomes too stiff, let stand at room temperature until slightly softened.)

2. For the cake layers: While the ganache chills, preheat the oven to 350°F. Butter the cake pans and line the bottom of each with a round of parchment or wax paper. Butter the paper and dust the pans with flour, knocking out excess flour.

3. Pulse the chestnuts with the flour, baking soda, and salt in a food processor until finely ground.

4. Beat the butter and brown sugar in a large bowl with an electric mixer at medium-high speed until pale and fluffy, about 3 minutes in a standing mixer or about 6 minutes with a handheld mixer. Add the eggs 1 at a time, beating well after each addition, then beat in the vanilla (the mixture will look a little

separated). Reduce the speed to low and add the flour mixture and sour cream alternately in 3 batches, beginning and ending with flour and mixing until just combined.

5. Divide the batter evenly among the pans and bake in the middle of the oven until pale golden and springy to the touch, about 30 minutes. Cool the cakes in their pans on racks, then invert onto racks and remove the parchment.

6. For the mousse and to assemble torte: Melt the butter and chocolate in a double boiler or a metal bowl set over a saucepan of barely simmering water, stirring until smooth, and stir in the cognac. Transfer to a bowl and chill, covered, stirring occasionally, until thickened to the consistency of softened butter, about 1 hour. (If the mixture becomes too stiff, let stand at room temperature until softened.)

7. Beat the cream in a bowl with cleaned beaters until it just holds soft peaks, then chill, covered, while beginning to assemble torte.

8. Put 1 cake layer on cardboard round on a rack set in a shallow baking pan (1 inch deep). Spread ½ cup ganache evenly over the top of the layer and sprinkle with all of the chopped marrons glacés. Top the marrons glacés with another ¼ cup ganache and cover with another cake layer.

9. Beat the egg whites with a pinch of salt in a bowl using cleaned beaters at medium-high speed until they just hold soft peaks. Add the sugar and beat at high speed until the whites just hold stiff peaks. Stir the whipped cream into the chocolate-cognac mixture, then stir in one third of the whites to lighten. Fold in the remaining whites gently but thoroughly. Spoon the mousse immediately onto the cake layer (it sets quickly), spreading evenly, then top with third cake layer. Chill the torte, covered, until the mousse layer is firm, about 1 hour. Keep the remaining ganache at a spreadable consistency at room temperature, chilling, covered, if it becomes too soft.

10. Glaze the cake: Reserve 1¼ cups ganache in a metal bowl, then spread the remainder over the top and sides of the torte to seal in crumbs. Chill until firm, about 1 hour.

11. Set the bowl of reserved ganache over a saucepan of barely simmering water, stirring until the ganache reaches a pourable consistency. Remove the bowl from the heat and cool 5 minutes. Pour the ganache evenly over the top of the torte, making sure it coats all sides. Shake the rack gently to smooth the glaze (let excess drip into the baking pan). Transfer the cake on cardboard to a cake stand or plate using 2 large heavy metal spatulas and chill until set. Garnish with caramelized chestnuts just before serving.

Notes: Bonneval chocolate is not currently available in the United States. Try using bittersweet chocolate from www.ghirardelli.com or www.lindt.com.

Candied chestnuts are often seasonal and around the holidays can be found at gourmet food stores such as Dean & DeLuca and Williams-Sonoma. At other times of year, try www.tienda.com.

The cake layers can be made 3 days ahead, cooled completely, then chilled, individually wrapped well in plastic wrap.

The ganache can be made 3 days ahead and chilled, covered. Let stand at room temperature 2 to 3 hours to soften to a spreadable consistency.

The torte can be assembled 2 days ahead and chilled, covered with a cake dome.

The egg whites in this recipe are not cooked. If salmonella is a problem in your area, you can use reconstituted powdered egg whites such as Just Whites.

OTHER EDIFYING EDIBLES

He will give to your land the early rain and the latter rain, that you may gather in your corn, and your wine, and your oil, and your hay out of the fields to feed your cattle, and that you may eat and be filled.

—DEUTERONOMY 11:14

ost monasteries once farmed for a living, and traces of this heritage remain at many of them: Mount Saint Mary's in New England still owns sheep (and a llama to guard them), while a monk at Gethsemani can tell you exactly how to get a distracted cow to focus on milking, although the abbey no longer has its own herd. The monks at Spencer Abbey once farmed, and they still use an old stone grain silo as their unusual confessional.

Thomas Merton was a monk at Gethsemani when the abbey was still a working farm. In his book *The Seven Storey Mountain*, he describes life there:

[During Easter season] we were planting peas and beans, and when it ended we were picking them. Then in May they cut the first crop of alfalfa in Saint Joseph's field, and from then on the novices were going out, morning and afternoon, in their long line, Indian file, straw hats on their heads, with pitchforks to hay fields in all quarters of the farm.

Of course, that was when Gethsemani had some two hundred monks and plenty of novices, but times have changed.

In Europe, monasteries including Westmalle in Belgium and Cîteaux in France still milk their own cows (the monks who care for the large herd at Westmalle know every cow by name), while others such as Tamié in the French Alps and Mont des Cats in French Flanders used to have cows but now buy milk from local farms.

There are many reasons abbeys in America and Europe have given up farming. Some, like Our Lady of Guadalupe (now in Oregon but previously in New Mexico) and Holy Spirit in Georgia, found that the land they tried to farm wasn't fertile. Others have had fewer vocations. Farming still made sense when an abbey like Gethsemani had more than two hundred monks after World War II, but vocations have dropped and Catholics are having fewer children (one monk at Gethsemani told a guest he was the youngest of eleven children!).

One thing that hasn't changed is the way that monks and nuns work, even if it is no longer on a farm. Saint Benedict says, "He who lives by the work of his own hands is truly a monk." Monasteries that once farmed now make candy, cheese, wine, beer, olive oil, jams, and holiday specialties like fruitcake. A majority of American monastery foods are made by Cistercians, but a growing number of other orders are also making food, including Dominicans (who make cinnamon bread in Wisconsin), Franciscans (who make cookies in New York state), and Carmelites (who make coffee in Wyoming).

Monasteries rarely use preservatives or artificial colors and flavors (except when they make traditional fruitcake). They also buy the freshest local ingredients they can find: the Abbey of Gethsemani uses Kentucky bourbon in its fruitcake and fudge, Mississippi Abbey in Iowa makes caramels with fresh cream and butter from local farms, and Holy Spirit Monastery puts Georgia peaches in its fudge.

Small abbeys that make food have a lot in common with family-owned businesses. They use the best ingredients, make artisanal products in small batches, and sometimes are forced to work with outdated equipment (an ornery machine for wrapping caramels springs to mind). Fortunately for the rest of us, ingenuity seems to flourish in monasteries, and monks and nuns invent equipment as often as they purchase it.

The foods that monks and nuns make may change over time, but their way of life remains timeless. From actively farming in the past to making food that ranges from fudge to fruitcake today, monasteries continue to adapt to the times they live in while following a way of life that is more than a thousand years old. It is a remarkable achievement. Thomas Merton once wrote that to choose a life of peace is itself a statement of one's position. By that measure these monks and nuns, who live in silence, have already spoken volumes.

The name "Trappist" comes from the Cistercian Abbey of La Trappe in Normandy, France, home to one of the great monastic reforms, in the late seventeenth century. When the French Revolution suppressed all the religious houses in 1790, the monks of La Trappe took refuge as a community in Switzerland, and after many hardships and wanderings they eventually returned to France in 1815 to refound the Abbey and the Congregation of La Trappe. This congregation flourished, and houses of Trappists were founded in Europe, the United States, and elsewhere, so that at present there are some one hundred houses of men and sixty of women throughout the world.

OUR LADY OF THE HOLY SPIRIT MONASTERY

NEAR CONYERS, GEORGIA

There's something about Holy Spirit Monastery that calls to mind Jurassic Park. Maybe it's the hundred-foot bald cypress trees that rise majestically from the lake at the foot of the hill or the flock of gargantuan geese who inhabit a sodden stretch of the shore. It could also be the way the guesthouse garden feels like a leftover patch of Eden, timeless and serene. In the heart of the garden sits a small stone well that is dotted with water lilies and snails; it's overlooked by a gentle lamb carved in bas-relief who maintains an unperturbed air amid a loud chorus of birds. Then there's the abbey's bonsai greenhouse, where a guest can't help but wonder if the tiny gnarled trees suffer from an inferiority complex in proximity to their soaring swamp cousins. Holy Spirit is real, but it feels like a place one might find in a dream.

The abbey's renowned fudge also invokes reveries, albeit of the culinary kind. The

Monastery of the Holy Spirit was founded in 1944 by Trappist monks from the Abbey of Gethsemani in Kentucky. Like Cîteaux, it was built on reclaimed swamp land with poor soil. The monks endured broiling-hot summers and bone-chilling winters, but they were always a prayer away from having enough money to finish building their church. Despite the odds grace took root, and a delicate church with Gothic flair began to emerge through the Georgia haze. The monks climbed scaffolds, poured concrete, and survived near-death accidents to build the church, but it's the beautiful stained glass that is most unforgettable—it makes the church look like a little Chartres on the bayou.

Georgia was better known for Baptists, peaches, and pecans than for Catholics when the Trappists arrived. They tried farming, but the soil could grow only hay. The monks needed another source of income and turned to making fudge (like their motherhouse,

Gethsemani). When one tastes the abbey's Southern Touch Fudge it feels like being gently kissed by a peach: it's made with peach brandy, real peaches, and pecans. Be sure to set the peach fudge aside long enough to try the abbey's other flavors, including chocolate, maple-walnut, and peanut butter. They're all made with fresh cream and butter.

Holy Spirit also has a line of gourmet foods that it markets under the Abbot's Table brand. Saint Benedict's rule says that guests and travelers should always be welcome at the abbot's table, and in that spirit the monks have created a variety of vinegars, hot sauces, marinades, mustards (available only in the gift shop), and, of course, fudge and fruitcake (available online and by mail order). In practice the abbot's table at Holy Spirit is more ascetic than these foods might suggest, but it's nice to think that Saint Benedict would be pleased.

Saint Benedict understood hospitality better than most, yet he chose to remove himself from the world and live in a cave near Subiaco. He felt a need to be apart. The need for solitude guided the Desert Fathers and led Saint Francis to another cave. Even the apostles needed time out, as when Jesus said to them, "Come aside by yourselves to a lonely place and rest awhile" (Mark 6:31). Guests make retreats to a monastery for many reasons, but they all share a need to be apart. Visitors to Holy Spirit have come for reasons ranging from addiction to simply wanting time to read. People on retreat and armchair travelers can plant a box of fudge at their elbows and get a flavor of solitude by reading *Come Aside Awhile*, a monk's reflections on his time as guestmaster (available in the gift shop).

Like all good things, retreats must come to an end. It can be a shock to leave an abbey only to find that a chorus of birds has been replaced by a cacophony of cell phones by the time one reaches the airport. Long before cell phones existed, Saint Bernard warned against pride. He said it breeds vanity and makes some people think they are better than others. Perhaps we can all strive to be a little more humble when we use our cell phones in a public space.

Fortunately, humility is not hard to find at this abbey. After all, what could be more humble than a bonsai plant that is less than a foot high? The monk who started Holy Spirit's bonsai greenhouse was a Yale-trained artist with a green thumb who set an example of humility even among his fellow monks. It's not hard to see why he liked bonsai; like faith itself, they require commitment, patience, and a good set of roots. Bonsai plants and supplies including Chinese mudmen and beautiful Tokoname pots are available in the greenhouse and online at www.bonsaimonk.com.

Despite their humble size, bonsai strive to be a perfect example of nature's beauty. They are the best little tree that they can be, and they are beautiful in a way that reaches one's heart as well as one's eye. People don't always come in perfect shapes and sizes, but we can all seek to be the best example of God's love that we can be. There's no better place to begin that journey than Holy Spirit.

When the monks first came to Georgia they raised cattle and pigs and sold hay. However, farm work was so labor-intensive and the land was so poor that they knew they would have to try something else. They baked bread for a while but the bakery was too small to support the abbey and the monks didn't have the resources to expand.

Meanwhile, the monks at the Abbey of Gethsemani in Kentucky, Holy Spirit's motherhouse, were doing a brisk business in bourbon fudge. The monks at Holy Spirit decided to give candymaking a try but added peach brandy instead of bourbon to their southern fudge, which quickly became a best-seller. The monks also make fruitcake.

The fudge helps to support the monastery, but the monks still rely on other sources of income, including the guesthouse and bonsai business.

Travel tip: The abbey can arrange transportation from the airport or train station by private car service for a fee. Guests must call 770-922-5083 in advance to reserve a ride.

FOOD PRODUCTS: Fudge, fruitcake, gourmet condiments

GUESTHOUSE: Yes, M/F

WEBSITE: www.abbeystore.com

ORDER: Phone, fax, e-mail, or write

PHONE: 800-592-5203

FAX: 770-860-9343

E-MAIL: service@abbeystore.org

Monastery of the Holy Spirit

The Abbey Store

2625 Highway 212 SW

Conyers, GA 30094

NEW SKETE MONASTERY

NEAR CAMBRIDGE, NEW YORK

A visitor to New Skete, nestled in the rolling Taconic mountains of upstate New York, might be forgiven for thinking that a wrong turn was taken along the way. During good weather visitors are as likely to be greeted by a wild-eyed corgi learning to sit, stay, and come on command as they are to encounter a monk dressed in full habit. But the monks here find that jeans and a T-shirt are the perfect outfit for training hapless pet owners and their wayward beasts. The monastery is most famous for breeding German shepherds, but its edible treats are equally worthy of accolades.

New Skete was founded in the 1960s by a group of Byzantine Rite Franciscan monks and Poor Clare nuns who later converted to the Orthodox Church of America. They settled on the summit of a gentle mountain, crowning it with a hand-built wooden church whose golden onion domes add a dollop of Russian soulfulness to the skyline. A larger church just up the hill greets guests with a frieze of saints painted on a Byzantine gold background that calls to mind the mosaics of Ravenna; however, these saints appear engaged in animated conversation rather than frozen for eternity like their Mediterranean counterparts.

If good food and camaraderie seem foreign to the popular notion of monastic life, New Skete will surprise and delight all visitors except those who seek a strict air of asceticism. Any community that makes cheesecake and a cheese spread spiked with enough sherry to cure a stiff cold is hardly inclined to don hair shirts or take meals through a slot in the door of a private cell (as Carthusians might).

A smokehouse on the grounds keeps the monks busy when they are not training man's best friend. The meats are smoked slowly over hickory wood, which yields a rich flavor that has won many regular customers. New Skete Farms offers bone-in and boneless hams, nitrite-free bacon, Canadian bacon, smoked turkey and chicken breast, chicken, smoked cheeses, cheese spreads, and a whole-grain pancake mix that is simply delicious with fresh blueberries added to the batter.

A balanced life is the staple diet here. It is Saint Benedict's *"Ora et labora"*—pray and work—laced with sherry, barking, laughter, and a meditation garden. There is also room for silence. Over a slice of cheesecake in the refectory on a recent visit, a nun worried that the constant need for noise and action in modern life leaves little room for exploring one's humanity. She especially worries about children who crave constant entertainment; when she was a girl, kids still enjoyed sitting on a blanket under the stars and soaking up the night sky in perfect silence. A New Skete monk also recommended silence to a visitor as a way of feeding one's inner life.

Fortunately, there are many ways for laypersons to practice silence and nurture their inner lives. Buddhist monks such as Thich Nhat Hanh and Buddhist centers around the country have introduced many Americans, including Catholic monks and nuns, to Zen mindfulness practices. Books such as Benedictine nun Mary Margaret Funk's *Thoughts Matter*, Trappist monk Basil Pennington's *Centering Prayer*, and Thich Nhat Hanh's *Zen Keys* are good resources and are available in many monastery gift shops. And there is no better place to read one of these than in New Skete's meditation garden! Trying to avoid distraction by the mini-plague of frogs that recently took up residence is good meditative practice.

There are also ways to feed the soul with tangible food that inspires divine thoughts. It's hard not to feel both humbled and uplifted when biting into a piece of Chocolate-Amaretto, Kahlúa, or Apple-Walnut Cheesecake made by New Skete nuns. There are flavors to suit every palate, including seasonal favorites like pumpkin in a ginger-vanilla crumb crust. The cakes can be served cold and savored much like a silky gelato or warm as freshly made pudding. At room temperature they strike a balanced note, neither too heavy nor too light, combining texture and flavor in a sensual mélange that is tasty enough to tempt even a pious person to ask for seconds. Cakes are shipped frozen and can be thawed in the refrigerator or stored in the freezer for up to a week.

So grab a blanket, some bread, and perhaps a bottle of wine, and share a picnic of New Skete smoked meats with friends. Or serve the monastery's natural bacon with some eggs for breakfast and a slice of cheesecake on the side. Wherever and with whomever these treats are enjoyed, try adding a few moments of silence to the menu so that the inner self will also be satisfied.

The monks who founded New Skete Monastery had hoped to be entirely self-sufficient and first tried growing all their own food. However, they weren't able to survive on farming alone, so they also worked as hired farmhands and even accepted some donations. They soon began making religious art such as icons and jewelry, and raising hogs and making sausages. They also added a smokehouse and started making ham and bacon (they no longer sell sausage).

The monks of New Skete are most famous for raising and training puppies. That business began when the monks owned their first pet German shepherd. Then they got another dog, and the two dogs had puppies. Pretty soon there was a demand for the monastery's puppies. The monks got serious about breeding German shepherds and realized they couldn't have puppies around without training them, so the next logical step was to master the fine art of dog training—and then a whole bunch of people really wanted their puppies. This remains the monastery's main source of income.

When the nuns of New Skete were founded, they originally earned their income by hiring themselves out to work as maids. Then a friend of the monastery gave the nuns a recipe for cheesecake. The nuns never looked back and have been making celestially inspired cheesecakes ever since.

FOOD PRODUCTS: Smoked meats, Canadian bacon, smoked cheese, cheese spreads, whole-grain pancake mix, cheesecake

GUESTHOUSE: Yes, M/F

WEBSITE: www.newsketemonks.com

ORDER: Phone, fax, e-mail, or write

MONKS

E-MAIL: monks@newskete.com

PHONE: 518-677-3928

FAX: 518-677-2373

GUESTHOUSE E-MAIL: monks@newskete.com (put "Guest" in the subject line)

New Skete Farms

P.O. Box 128

Cambridge, NY 12816

NUNS

E-MAIL: nuns@newskete.com

PHONE: 518-677-3810

FAX: 518-677-3001

GUESTHOUSE E-MAIL: nuns@newskete.com (put "Sister Rebecca" in the subject line)

The Nuns of New Skete

343 Ash Grove Road

Cambridge, NY 12816

Monastic life is communal; however, individual talents are not suppressed. Many monastery gift shops reflect the artistic talents of individual members of the community. For example, New Skete and Saint Joseph's Abbey in Massachusetts both have talented icon painters (St. Joseph Chapel in lower Manhattan commissioned a New Skete nun to paint a commemorative icon after 9/11), while Saint Hildegard in Germany has a nun who makes custom-designed jewelry and a nun at Mississippi Abbey in Iowa makes lovely handcrafted pottery.

Stop by New Skete's gift shop for greeting cards that reproduce the nuns' icons and Christmas cards that picture the most adorable German shepherd puppies this side of heaven!

SUGGESTED ITINERARY: UPSTATE NEW YORK

Upstate New York is a surprisingly good place to get a taste of monastic life. Here are some suggestions for building your itinerary:

GENESEE ABBEY

3258 RIVER ROAD

PIFFARD, NY 14533

WWW.MONKSBREAD.COM

877-264-6785

What could be better soul food than a loaf of bread baked by monks? The Trappist monks at Genesee Abbey have spent decades perfecting their wholesome bread recipe and now offer seven flavors (available in the gift shop and online). Don't worry if you can't choose which one to try first—just get the Monks' Choice sampler. And if bread alone doesn't satisfy your soul, contact the monks to schedule a spiritual retreat (take Amtrak to Rochester and then drive, or take a Greyhound or Trailways bus to Genesee, and the monks will pick you up).

NEW SKETE MONASTERY

NEW SKETE MONKS

P.O. BOX 128

CAMBRIDGE, NY 12816

WWW.NEWSKETEMONKS.COM

518-677-3928

NEW SKETE NUNS

343 ASH GROVE ROAD

CAMBRIDGE, NY 12816

PHONE: 518-677-3810

One taste of the New Skete Nuns' cheesecake and you may find yourself wanting to move to upstate New York rather than just visit. Fortunately, visitors can take some cheesecake home with them, along with the smoked meats, Canadian bacon, and delicious cheese spreads made by the monks. For anyone who indulges in too much cheesecake, there are miles of hiking trails here, and the monks and nuns both run small guesthouses. Saratoga Springs and Cambridge are an easy drive from the monastery, and each offers weary pilgrims a chance to stay in historic bed and breakfasts on the way to or from New Skete.

OUR LADY OF THE RESURRECTION MONASTERY

246 BARMORE ROAD

LA GRANGEVILLE, NY 12540

Brother Victor-Antoine d'Avila Latourette once told a reporter that "what matters to the monk is not so much how his life unfolds, but that he finds the place where God wants him to be." God clearly wanted Brother Victor to be in upstate New York, where his talents have blossomed like the herbs and flowers that he plants in his garden. He also raises chickens and sheep, makes vinegars, tapenades, and jams, and somehow still finds time to write masterful cookbooks. He is the only monk left at this rustic monastery, but he gets some volunteer help from Vassar students. If you want to volunteer, write to him. Better yet, stop by the monastery on a weekend afternoon when the gift shop is open and meet him in person. (Poughkeepsie is the nearest train station.) Just remember the rule for buying monastic products, especially with only one monk here to make them—when they're gone, they're gone! Be patient, and pray for vocations.

SPROUT CREEK FARM

34 LAUER ROAD

POUGHKEEPSIE, NY 12603

WWW.SPROUTCREEKFARM.ORG

MARKET AND CREAMERY 845-485-9885

Sprout Creek Farm was started by Sister Margo of the Society of the Sacred Heart (www.rscjinternational.org), who still runs the place, although secular workers now make the farmstead cheeses (try the fresh ricotta!). The farm educates thousands of schoolchildren each year about sustainable farming and rents out a cottage for private retreats. (Take Amtrak or Metro-North Commuter Railroad from New York to Pough-keepsie, then grab a taxi to the farm.)

The gift shop sells cheeses made with milk from the farm's cows and goats and gourmet gifts such as sea salts. Many of the locals who work here have studied at the Culinary Institute of America (CIA) in Hyde Park. So if you're looking for a weekend getaway that combines culinary and spiritual pursuits, why not stay at Sprout Creek's cottage? From there you can drive to Brother Victor's monastery for prayers and the gift shop, then stop at CIA's Apple Pie Bakery Café (www.ciachef.edu/restaurants) on the way home.

You know a truly great chef is at work when you use one of his recipes for pickling and it changes the way you see pickled foods forever. If that chef is Gray Kunz, who happens to be a fan of Brother Victor's artisanal vinegars, then the result is a recipe that is truly sublime. Chef Kunz has already made his unforgettable mark in the culinary world—formerly at Lespinasse and Café Gray in New York—but it's safe to assume that the best is yet to come from this innovative chef. In the meantime, cooks can content themselves with this versatile recipe. Kunz suggests using the pickle with grilled meats or to spice up a summer green salad. This recipe has been adapted from The Elements of Taste *by Gray Kunz and Peter Kaminsky.*

2 cups Brother Victor's cider vinegar (see Note) or distilled white vinegar

1 cup sugar

Zest of 2 lemons

2 cups thinly sliced papaya (2 smallish papayas)

1 tablespoon Short Rib Spice Mix (recipe follows)

Bring the vinegar and sugar to a boil in a small saucepan and stir to dissolve the sugar. Add the zest. Toss the papaya with the spice mix. Pour the vinegar mixture over the papaya and refrigerate until needed.

Note: Chef Kunz likes to cook with Brother Victor's artisanal vinegars, which can be purchased at the abbey gift shop at Brother Victor's monastery, Our Lady of the Resurrection. It is located near Millbrook, New York.

SHORT RIB SPICE MIX

1 tablespoon whole allspice

1 teaspoon whole cloves

4 teaspoons coriander seeds

1 bay leaf

1 tablespoon cumin seeds

1 tablespoon Szechuan peppercorns (see Note)

1 tablespoon black peppercorns

1 tablespoon ground cinnamon

Kosher salt

Toast the allspice, cloves, coriander, bay leaf, cumin, and Szechuan pepper in a dry skillet over medium heat until fragrant. Add the black peppercorns and grind in a spice grinder or mortar until the mixture is medium-fine. Put the spice mix in a clean container with a tight-fitting lid. Add the cinnamon and a pinch of salt and mix well.

Note: Szechuan peppercorns (also known as Sichuan peppercorns) can be found at Chinese and Asian markets. To purchase them online, visit www.penzeys.com or www .kalustyans.com.

As a guest on retreat at New Skete, a recent convert to vegetarianism felt her resolve weaken when she caught a whiff of smoked hickory in the air. The monks make hickory-smoked turkey, ham, bacon, and cheese. Vegetarians with more willpower can stick to the smoked cheese, cheese spreads, and cheesecake made by the New Skete nuns, while carnivores can simply give thanks. The monks kindly shared this recipe.

1 (4- to 4½-pound) boneless pork loin roast, trimmed

Salt and freshly ground black pepper

3 cloves garlic, minced

1½ tablespoons chopped fresh rosemary

1 pound sliced New Skete smoked bacon (see Note) or other hickory-smoked
   bacon

1 cup low-sodium chicken broth

½ cup dry white wine

1. Place the roast, fat side up, in a roasting pan, remove any strings, pat dry, and season generously with salt and pepper. Rub the garlic and rosemary all over. Lay the bacon slices crosswise over the loin, overlapping slightly, and tuck the ends of the bacon underneath the loin. Cover and refrigerate for 8 hours or overnight.

2. Put an oven rack in the middle position and preheat the oven to 350°F. Roast the pork until a thermometer registers 150°F, about 1½ hours. Transfer the roast to a cutting board and tent with foil. Let the roast rest for at least 20 minutes. (The temperature will continue to rise slightly as the roast rests.)

3. Meanwhile, pour the pan juices into a glass measuring cup, skim the fat

from the juices, and discard. Return the pan juices to the roasting pan. Set the roasting pan over two burners. Add the broth and wine and bring to a boil over medium-high heat, scraping any browned bits from the bottom of the pan. Reduce the liquid by half, then add in any meat juices that have accumulated on the cutting board. Continue to reduce until slightly thickened, then season with salt and pepper.

4. Slice the roast and serve with the juice on the side.

Note: Visit www.newsketemonks.com to order New Skete Farms smoked bacon.

SAINT JOSEPH'S ABBEY, AKA SPENCER ABBEY

NEAR SPENCER, MASSACHUSETTS

A guest who arrives at Saint Joseph's on a winter's eve is struck by the beauty of the place despite the cold. It feels like a charming European village made of stone. The snow only makes this old farmstead more beautiful, softening the rough stone edges of a former grain silo that has found a second life as the monks' confessional. Any guest who happens to be here during a blizzard will notice how peaceful the place remains, thanks to a system of connected walkways that protects one from the elements. In fact, there's something about the snow, stones, and stained glass that makes Spencer feel special, as though it were more ancient than its years. On a recent visit a guest couldn't shake the feeling that she might turn a corner in the cloisters and find Saint Bernard, donning his choir robe.

Saint Joseph's may feel timeless, but it was founded in 1950 by monks who arrived from Canada via Rhode Island. It belongs to the Order of Cistercians of the Strict Observance, and the monks can trace their family tree back to the famous Abbey of La Trappe in France. The abbey's land was once a working farm, and the monks used to pray in a converted hayloft while they were building the church out of reclaimed fieldstones. It was worth the effort: this abbey is as beautiful by day as it is by night, when it glows like a medieval castle.

The guesthouse is made of unusual bricks that were overcooked; they lend it a fairy-tale quality, as though it were made of gingerbread that someone forgot to take out of the oven. It was designed by an architect with an eye for antiques, and his eclectic style includes cast-iron lamps, camelback sofas, and terra-cotta reliefs. The building's shape is as unusual as its appearance. Three wings of rooms form a triangle around a courtyard garden that is framed with distinctive arches. It's a guesthouse that is as charming as it is popular, so be patient if it is fully booked for retreats.

New England is the birthplace of the Concord grape, so it's fitting that Saint Joseph's makes preserves, jams, jellies, and conserves. Ephraim Wales Bull cultivated the Concord grape right here in Massachusetts, where he owned a farm and planted more than 20,000 seedlings! When he wasn't furiously planting and growing grapes, Bull must have had some interesting chats with his neighbors, who included Ralph Waldo Emerson and Henry David Thoreau.

It took a man from New Jersey to turn Bull's grape into an American legend: Dr. Thomas Bramwell Welch was a Methodist, and he first made Concord grape juice as a substitute for wine in Communion (Methodists didn't like the idea of using alcohol in church). Welch did a thriving business selling grape juice to churches, and in 1923 he introduced his famous grape jelly.

Unlike Methodists, Catholics prefer wine to grape juice when they take Holy Communion; the monks even put wine in their jelly, which comes in sherry, port, and burgundy flavors. Saint Joseph's makes twenty-eight flavors in total, ranging from classics like blueberry, strawberry, and orange marmalade to bold new flavors like hot pepper, ginger, and pomegranate. All Trappist preserves are made in small, kettle-cooked batches that allow the monks to carefully control quality. The abbey buys the best fruit it can find from local, national, and even international growers (for example, apricots are sometimes imported from Australia) and uses no artificial ingredients. Whichever flavor one prefers, these preserves taste like heaven.

The jam factory is buzzing with energy although the monks are mostly silent. The monks' commitment to quality would make Ephraim Wales Bull proud. A monk whizzes by a guest on his way to run quality tests on a fresh batch sample. Other monks look like bees tending a hive as they hover over large kettles of fruit that are cooked at precise temperatures and times. A third monk stands guard with fierce concentration as jars of jam march past on a conveyor belt; he removes any flawed fruit, leaving only gleaming ruby-red preserves (the monks follow different recipes according to the day of the week).

The monks work hard, but making preserves is part of a well-balanced life. It's amazing to see the same monks go from a busy factory, where they dress in jeans and sneakers, to church, where their long white choir robes make them appear as if they were floating rather than walking. The factory is noisy, but in here one hears only the monks, who sing like angels. It's no surprise that this abbey is still drawing vocations.

One of the monks gave a visitor a homily to read. It was about how the Devil tempted Jesus in the desert, where Jesus fasted for forty days. The Devil knew that Jesus must be hungry, and he suggested that Jesus turn some rocks into a loaf of bread. Jesus, however, replied that we are not sustained by food alone but also by the word of God—in other words, we are nourished by our spiritual lives as much as by our culinary ones. It's nice to think that Saint Joseph's will be around for as long as men answer a call to feed their souls as well as their stomachs. Meanwhile, the rest of us can soothe our hunger with a slice of toast and some heavenly jam from Saint Joseph's Abbey.

The monks of Saint Joseph's tried farming when they first arrived in Massachusetts (their land was once a working farm) and even had to pray in a converted hayloft until the abbey church was built. They raised cows and grew crops but soon realized farming wasn't profitable enough to cover their bills.

One year a bumper crop of mint grew in the monastery garden. A monk turned it into a batch of mint jelly that quickly sold out in the gift shop (in those days the monks' diet was so ascetic that they were not permitted to eat the jelly themselves). The monks began experimenting with their jelly recipe and now make twenty-eight flavors of jams, jellies, preserves, and conserves (the latter contain nuts).

As members of the Holy Rood Guild (http://holyroodguild.com), they also make handcrafted liturgical vestments for priests.

FOOD PRODUCTS: Preserves (jams, jellies, conserves)

GUESTHOUSE: Yes, M/F

WEBSITE: www.spencerabbey.org

ORDER: Place orders through Monastery Greetings, www.monasterygreetings
.com, or Heaven Gourmet, www.heavengourmet.com.

E-MAIL: info@monasterygreetings.com

PHONE: 800-472-0425 (toll-free)

GUESTHOUSE PHONE: 508-885-8710, 9:00–11:00 a.m. and 1:30–7:30 p.m.
(Reservations are not accepted by voice mail or e-mail.)
Saint Joseph's Abbey
167 North Spencer Road
Spencer, MA 01562-1233

CRÊPES SAINT-GUÉNOLÉ WITH
SEVILLE ORANGE MARMALADE

Saint Guénolé, known in English as Winwaloe, founded the Monastery of Landévennec in the fifth century. His heritage was Cornish, but he was born in Brittany. This recipe is named in his honor, and it combines the best traditions of France and the British Isles in a delicious crêpe with marmalade. It is adapted from Brother Victor-Antoine d'Avila-Latourrette's book From a Monastery Kitchen: The Classic Natural Foods Cookbook.

3 large eggs (for more tender crêpes, use only the yolks)

1 cup whole milk

1½ cups all-purpose flour

5 tablespoons unsalted butter, melted

2 tablespoons orange liqueur

1 tablespoon sugar

2 tablespoons finely grated orange zest (from 2 oranges)

1 cup Saint Joseph's Trappist Preserves Seville orange marmalade (see Note) or
    other artisanal marmalade

1. Beat the eggs or egg yolks well in a large bowl. Whisk in the milk and ½ cup water. Gradually whisk in the flour until smooth, and then whisk in 4 tablespoons of the melted butter. Strain the batter through a fine-mesh sieve into a bowl, cover, and refrigerate for at least 2 hours or overnight to let rest.

2. Just before using, stir in the orange liqueur, sugar, and orange zest.

3. Heat a 7-inch crêpe pan or 8-inch nonstick skillet over medium heat until hot, then very lightly brush with some of the remaining melted butter. Do not use

too much butter or the crêpes will be greasy. Pour in just enough batter to lightly coat the bottom of the pan (about 3 tablespoons), tilting and rotating the pan as you pour to evenly distribute the batter. Cook one side until light golden, about 1½ minutes, then loosen the edges and flip using a spatula. Cook the other side lightly, about another minute.

4. Transfer the crêpe to a clean work surface and spread 1 teaspoon marmalade on one side, then fold into quarters. Continue making and assembling crêpes, brushing the pan very lightly with butter as necessary, until you use up all the batter. You may not need to use all of the melted butter. Stack the crêpes as finished and cover with wax paper. Serve warm.

Note: Visit www.monasterygreetings.com or www.heavengourmet.com to purchase Trappist Preserves, including Seville orange marmalade.

Quick Apple Cake
with Ginger Preserves

This cake captures the essence of autumn with its apple and ginger flavors, but it's good enough to eat at any time of year. Brother Victor-Antoine d'Avila-Latourrette kindly shared this recipe. It's adapted from his book From a Monastery Kitchen: The Classic Natural Foods Cookbook.

Unsalted butter for greasing the pan

2 large eggs

⅓ cup whole milk

¾ cup whole wheat flour

6 tablespoons granulated or light brown sugar

2 teaspoons baking powder

Pinch of salt

⅓ cup canola or vegetable oil

2 apples, peeled, cored, and cut into ¼-inch slices

⅓ cup Saint Joseph's ginger preserves, quince jelly, or cranberry conserves (see Note)

1. Preheat the oven to 350°F. Grease an 8-inch square baking pan and set aside.

2. Beat the eggs well in a large bowl, then add the milk and whisk to combine. In a separate bowl, whisk together the flour, sugar, baking powder, and salt and add to the egg mixture. Beat in the oil. The batter should be thick. Scrape the batter into the prepared pan and smooth the top.

3. Arrange the apple slices on the cake, inserting their cored edges into the batter over the entire surface. Bake for 35 minutes, then remove from the oven.

Drop spoonfuls of preserves over the cake top and gently smooth the surface. Return to the oven and bake until the cake is golden and glazed, another 5 to 7 minutes.

4. Let the cake cool slightly in the pan on a wire rack. This rustic cake can be served in the pan.

Note: Visit www.monasterygreetings.com or www.heavengourmet.com to purchase Saint Joseph's preserves, jellies, and conserves.

Brother Simeon's Lentil and Artichoke Stew

Brother Simeon Leiva of Saint Joseph's Abbey in Spencer, Massachusetts, shared this hearty lentil stew recipe. It's especially good for keeping warm in the middle of a winter snowstorm. We include it here because we think it goes well with toast and preserves on the side, but we also suggest using olive oil from Ganagobie Abbey in France or your favorite extra-virgin olive oil. This stew has a pleasantly strong taste—feel free to adjust it as you please.

1 pound green lentils, picked over, rinsed, and drained

4 cups chicken broth

½ cup extra-virgin olive oil from Ganagobie Abbey (see Note) or other young
　　fresh fruity olive oil, plus extra for drizzling

1 bell pepper, cut into thin strips (a combination of green, red, and yellow
　　peppers is attractive)

1 medium onion, finely chopped (about 1½ cups)

1 (14-ounce) can quartered artichoke hearts, drained

2 tablespoons minced garlic

3 tablespoons chopped fresh parsley

2 teaspoons ground coriander

½ teaspoon ground cloves

¾ cup tomato-based vegetable juice (Brother Simeon uses V8 Juice)

Salt and freshly ground black pepper

1. Put the lentils and the chicken broth in a large pot and bring to a boil over high heat. Drizzle a little olive oil over the lentils to keep them loose. When they begin to boil, reduce the heat to maintain a simmer and cover the pot.

2. Meanwhile, in a medium saucepan combine the peppers, onions, artichoke hearts, garlic, parsley, coriander, and cloves. Add the ½ cup of oil, the vegetable juice, and enough water to cover the contents well. Bring to a boil over high heat, then reduce the heat to maintain a simmer.

3. When the peppers are very tender, about 20 minutes, add the artichoke mixture to the lentils. Mix until well combined and season with salt and pepper to taste. Cover the pot and simmer until the lentils are tender. (Cooking time varies for lentils depending on how old they are; it can take anywhere from 20 to 45 minutes until they are tender.) Stir well from time to time to keep lentils from sticking to bottom of pot. Cook until the stew reaches desired thickness; longer cooking over low heat produces a thicker stew.

Note: Extra-virgin olive oil from Ganagobie Abbey is not currently available in the United States. You can substitute your favorite extra-virgin olive oil.

OUR LADY OF GUADALUPE ABBEY

NEAR LAFAYETTE, OREGON

From the minute one spies the vast selection of J. R. R. Tolkien books on the shelves of
this abbey's bookstore, one instinctively knows: This is a good place to find your inner
hobbit. This suspicion is further confirmed when one learns that this monastery is
famous for its brandy-soaked fruitcake, delicious date-nut cake, and wine warehouse that
stores some of Oregon's finest vintages; after all, no one loves good food and drink more
than a hobbit. Throw in a meditation center worthy of the greatest wizard and a forest so

beautiful that it brings out the high-minded Elf in us all, and one has surely found a hobbit's version of paradise.

Our Lady of Guadalupe was founded in 1948 and belongs to the Order of Cistercians of the Strict Observance, also known as Trappists; the monks (who came from the same monastic community in Rhode Island that also founded Saint Joseph's in Massachusetts) first settled in New Mexico. When they moved to Oregon in 1955 they kept their southwestern name, which was inspired by Mexico's patron saint, but traded farming for woodworking. The monks are certified green foresters and once made wooden church pews to support their abbey. When they decided to make cakes and warehouse wine instead, hobbits everywhere rejoiced.

Monks often have a good sense of humor and apparently so do their customers. One customer got the idea of taking a Guadalupe fruitcake to the South Pole and sending a photo of it to the monks. That photo inspired others and the monastery's fruitcake has since made its way to a temple in Thailand and the Great Wall of China. The monks use the photos in their media kit.

Quite a few monasteries make fruitcake, partly because it requires a modest amount of labor and also because fruitcake has a good shelf life. Guadalupe's classic fruitcake is

jam-packed with fruit and nuts, including bright red cherries and golden pineapple; the batter is so thick that the monks have to mix it by hand as no electric mixer has withstood the challenge. The dense, moist cake can be cut with a sharp knife (a bread knife works well) into paper-thin slices that have been likened to stained glass when they are held up to the light. Guadalupe's cakes are soaked with a generous measure of brandy and are nothing like the desiccated holiday treats that have given fruit-cake a bad name. Monastery fruitcakes are a hot Christmas gift, so be sure to place holiday orders early.

Some fruitcake aficionados swear that it pairs well with red wine. Oregon is as good a place as any to put this theory to the test. Guadalupe Abbey lies in the heart of the Wil-lamette Valley's wine country, about an hour and a half drive from Portland. The state's Pinots began winning prestigious competitions in France years ago and French tourists are a common sight. Meanwhile, every local one meets seems to have a connection to the wine industry, whether they've helped with a harvest, run a B&B for wine tourists, or even own a vineyard. It's wine-fever country.

It's also forest country. The monks manage about seven hundred acres of woods where vast stands of conifers soar to heights unfamiliar to shire-dwellers, and a passerby can't help giggling at the sight of patches of moss so thick that they can be stroked like a pet cat. The verdant undergrowth along the Saint Benedict Trail is sprinkled with raindrops that twinkle like a carpet of diamonds when the sun peeks through, while enormous ferns cascade down the steep slopes of a trail that leads up the mountain to a breathtaking view of the valley; along a third trail a hiker crosses a slender footbridge that is covered with something like shamrocks and is fit for an elf. One half expects the trees in these enchanted woods to come to life and start walking and talking, or at least to encounter an Ent or two.

Even the monastery's charming guest quarters remind one of a favorite childhood tree house, thanks in part to a maze of suspended wooden walkways that links them; the houses perch like storks next to a pond that is home to ducks and toads and whose mir-rored surface is rarely disturbed except by an occasional gust of wind. There's no need to set an alarm here, as a chorus of birds wakes visitors at the first hint of dawn.

Dawn is the perfect time of day to read and contemplate. One can sit in a rocking chair in one's room and gaze out at the pond and forest while reading from J. R. R. Tolkien, Thomas Merton, or Thich Nhat Hanh (all are available in the bookstore). Or one can read Saint Thérèse of Lisieux (whose photo hangs in the monastery's book bindery) and contemplate just how different the world might be if everyone who visits a monastery were to practice a thousand little acts of kindness when they go home.

For young men who wish to stay longer the monks offer a thirty-day Monastic Life Retreat several times a year. There is no charge for the retreat since each participant earns his room and board through his daily work with the monks. Whether a young man is a Tolkien fan, feels he has a calling to serve God, or simply loves to hike, he may wish to contemplate the words of Isaac of Nineveh, a seventh-century Syrian monk who is quoted in the Monastic Life Retreat brochure:

> Silence will unite you to God . . . In the beginning we have to force ourselves to be silent. But then from our very silence is born something that draws us into deeper silence.
>
> May God give you an experience of this "something" that is born of silence.

May all of us who are not called to the monastic life still experience this "something" that is born of silence, perhaps while munching on a slice of fruitcake and raising a glass of Oregon wine in a toast to the monks.

Necessity is the mother of invention, and that is especially true for monasteries. Guadalupe Abbey was founded in New Mexico, but the monks didn't have much luck with farming there. When they moved to Oregon, they started a business making wooden church pews. However, demand for pews among Protestants and Catholics has steadily declined, especially since Vatican II, when some Catholic churches began experimenting with using separate chairs instead of fixed pews to seat the faithful.

Today the monks make fruitcake and date-nut cakes. They also run a book-binding business, manage a warehouse for some of Oregon's finest wines, and are certified "green" foresters.

FOOD PRODUCTS: Fruitcake, date-nut cake

GUESTHOUSE: Yes, M/F

WEBSITE: www.trappistabbey.org

ORDER: Online store, phone, e-mail, or write

E-MAIL: bakery@trappistabbey.org

PHONE: 800-294-0105

GUESTHOUSE PHONE: 503-852-0107, 9:00 a.m.–noon weekdays (Reservations are not accepted by voice mail or e-mail.)

Our Lady of Guadalupe Trappist Abbey

9200 N.E. Abbey Road

Lafayette, OR 97127

When it comes to fruitcake, maybe you can have your cake and eat it too. One day an unsuspecting homeowner discovered a long-lost fruitcake beneath a bed. It turned out to be from Holy Cross Abbey in the Blue Ridge Mountains of Virginia. When the homeowner called the monks they immediately sent a new cake in exchange for the old one, and then set about trying to determine the age of the latter. Using some basic fruitcake forensics—packaging, consistency, and yes, even taste—the monks determined that the mystery cake was about twelve years old!

Of course, the monks don't recommend waiting that long to eat one of their fruitcakes, but they kindly shared some clues as to what makes their fruitcake taste so good—and stay fresh. The abbey's recipe uses a ratio of fruit and nuts to batter of about three to one; the less batter a fruitcake has, the longer its shelf life. Ernie Polanskas, a secular master baker who works with the monks, says the cakes also get "a full jigger of brandy" and are covered with a honey glaze that seals in moisture as soon as they leave the oven. Nevertheless, Ernie says the best time to eat Holy Cross fruitcake is when it arrives!

Visit the abbey's online store at www.monasteryfruitcake.org for fruitcake, creamed honey, and truffles, and be sure to try the fraters—fruitcake slices dipped in dark chocolate. The abbey also offers retreats for men and women.

MONASTERY FRUITCAKE AT A GLANCE

GENESEE ABBEY

www.geneseeabbey.org

Genesee makes a two-pound cake that comes in a flavor for every palate, including rum and burgundy wine (both with alcohol), coconut almond (contains no nuts), vanilla, and butterscotch. The monastery is a peaceful oasis in upstate New York about a half-hour south of Rochester, and it offers silent retreats for men and women. The abbey is also famous for its bread (available on the website, at www.monksbread.com).

ASSUMPTION ABBEY

www.assumptionabbey.org

Assumption Abbey makes a two-pound fruitcake that is dark, rich, and moist. The abbey's recipe was developed with the help of a famous French chef, Jean-Pierre Augé, who once worked for the Duke and Duchess of Windsor. The abbey offers excellent hiking opportunities among the lovely woods and streams of the Missouri Ozarks, and it welcomes men and women for retreats.

HOLY CROSS ABBEY

www.hcava.org

Holy Cross makes a traditional fruitcake that weighs in at two pounds, four ounces and is flavored with a good measure of brandy; it's also chock-full of fruits, nuts, and candied citrus peel. The abbey guesthouse is in a stunning location in the Blue Ridge Mountains of Virginia, only about an hour from Washington, D.C., and it welcomes men and women for retreats.

OUR LADY OF GUADALUPE

www.trappistabbey.org

Guadalupe makes a traditional brandy-soaked one-pound fruitcake. Fans say that a slice of this cake—which is densely packed with cherries, pineapple, and nuts—looks like stained glass when it's held up to the light. The abbey is located in the heart of Oregon's wine country and has miles of hiking trails. Men and women are welcome for retreats.

HOLY SPIRIT ABBEY

www.HolySpiritMonasteryGifts.com

Holy Spirit's fruitcake is made in Georgia under the expert guidance of Brother Patrick, who adds a delicious southern touch to the abbey's cakes: they are aged with peach brandy and sherry. The result is a moist, dense cake packed with pecans, peaches, pineapple, raisins, dates, and cherries.

MONASTERY OF OUR LADY OF GANAGOBIE

NEAR SISTERON IN ALPES-DE-HAUTE-PROVENCE, FRANCE

A visitor may have trouble deciding which is better here, the spiritual retreat or the luxury skin care products. However, as lovely as this monastery's fine soaps, lotions, and scented oils are, it is the place itself that rejuvenates a guest. The menu of things to do here includes gazing at a valley that Cézanne would have loved, hiking with only a soaring hawk for company, and catching a sunrise so beautiful it seems as if the earth had been born that very day. And then there's the monastery's sublime Romanesque church whose beauty is best summed up in the words of an awestruck Parisian tourist: *C'est magnifique!*

The Monastery of Our Lady of Ganagobie was founded in 965 by the Abbey of Cluny and belongs to the Order of Saint Benedict. Ganagobie remained a Cluny priory until the French Revolution, when the monks were exiled and the church suffered serious damage; since the revolution Ganagobie has owed its history to another abbey—the Abbey of Saint-Pierre de Solesmes—and to a remarkable priest named Dom Prosper Guéranger. Even as an entire generation was coming of age in France without a good understanding of the Catholic liturgy or monastic life, Dom Guéranger felt called to be a monk when he was just twenty-seven years old. He moved into an abandoned priory with a few other priests and they began to live according to the Rule of Saint Benedict; the priory soon became an abbey, and the abbey became the motherhouse of an entire family of monasteries, the Congrégation de Solesmes, which includes Ganagobie.

Dom Guéranger undertook an ambitious project to restore Gregorian chant to its original melodies and texts. Gregorian chants are monophonic vocal chants that are sung in Latin and use texts from the Bible and especially the Psalms (the Kyrie Eleison is a famous example). They were first sung in Roman churches in the fifth and sixth centuries and were learned by ear. Over many centuries the aural tradition faded, the texts were altered, and the interpretive instructions that had accompanied the music were lost; these changes dampened the beauty and spiritual power of the original chants. The monks of Solesmes began a painstaking process of gathering and comparing chant manuscripts from libraries all across Europe, sifting and winnowing until they had discerned a universal version for each chant (for more on the history of Gregorian Chant, see www.solesmes.com). The fruits of their labor can still be heard at Ganagobie, especially at Compline, when the monks sing a lyrical Salve Regina by candlelight.

The monastery's Romanesque church is one of the most magical places on earth to hear Gregorian chant. It was built in the twelfth century and has a strikingly austere form that is almost free of windows, but the effect is transcendent rather than gloomy. The church's façade is almost whimsical with its scalloped arches, carved columns, and a row of squat bearded apostles whose legs dangle above the entrance. Inside visitors will want to check out the twelfth-century mosaics (the best time to view them is after Sunday Mass); this fantastic menagerie depicted in bold black, white, and red tiles includes a medieval version of an elephant—who is Ganagobie's mascot—and a lion who stares straight out at guests as though he were eyeing his next meal.

Meals in the rustic dining room are mercifully less predatory and offer guests their first chance to taste Ganagobie's delicious jams and honeys. The jam comes in Mediterranean flavors such as apricot-almond, and fig, and even watermelon, while the honey comes in flavors such as lavender and acacia. The monks used to make the honey themselves before moving to Ganagobie but discovered that the high plateau here was too dry for bees; they now commission local producers in the valley below to make honey, jams, a delicious honey-flavored *pâtes de fruits*, and a juice made of sea buckthorn berries (buckthorn is an ancient Mediterranean bush whose berries are exceptionally high in nutritional value). It is the monks, however, who harvest the olives for their very own brand of olive oil, which is currently sold only in the gift shop.

Other products that are made for the monastery using the monks' expert knowledge of plants and herbs include fine soaps, shampoos, and creams made with natural ingredients such as sage, eucalyptus, rosemary, cloves, and shea butter. There's also a line of scented oils here, including a refreshing one that is made with lavender grown by the monks; it captures the very essence of Provence in a bottle and is sure to bring sweet dreams when sprinkled on one's pillow.

Stones are the preferred building material in Provence and they are ubiquitous at Ganagobie; there are cobblestones beneath one's feet and stone walls everywhere one

looks. After lunch one can sit on a bench by the retreat house—the bench is made of stone, naturally—and sip coffee while chatting with other guests (note: on a recent visit of mine, the monks and other guests here spoke only French) or stroll past the orchard to see the lovely stone shepherd's hut with its conical roof. The best stones here by far are the ones that crop up on the edge of the woods, where one can sit and watch the Durance Valley turn gold in the late-afternoon sun.

No matter how often you've seen reproductions of Vincent van Gogh's *Starry Night* on T-shirts and tote bags, nothing prepares you for the real night sky in Provence. It is as though crushed diamonds had been suspended above your head. It's nice to sit under this velvety mantle and contemplate what makes Ganagobie so welcoming. The word "tolerant" comes up time and again when guests describe the monks, and maybe tolerance is what's missing most from life beyond these walls; in a world fueled by envy, people are no longer content with being themselves, much less accepting of others. Open your heart to tolerance here, and be glad that there is no one rich, powerful, or famous enough to buy the sky above Ganagobie.

FOOD PRODUCTS: Olive oil, jams, *pâtes de fruits*

GUESTHOUSE: Yes, M/F

WEBSITE: www.ndganagobie.com

ORDER: E-mail, phone, or write

E-MAIL: boutique@ndganagobie.com

NOTE: For international calls, first dial 011 from the United States or 00 from Europe, then 33 for France, followed by the local phone number listed below; if the local number begins with a zero, drop it when dialing from abroad.

PHONE: (0)4 92 68 15 97

GUESTHOUSE E-MAIL: p.hotelier@ndganagobie.com

GUESTHOUSE PHONE: (0)4 92 68 12 10

Our Lady of Ganagobie Abbey

Le Prieuré

04310 Ganagobie

France

Brother Victor-Antoine d'Avila-Latourrette's palate was refined in the south of France, where he was raised. It is the way he combines monastic simplicity with the flavors of Provence that makes this recipe special. It has been adapted from his book A Monastery Kitchen: The Classic Natural Foods Cookbook.

16 large garlic cloves, minced or pressed through a garlic press

¼ cup extra-virgin olive oil from Ganagobie Abbey (see Note) or other young,

    fresh, fruity olive oil

1 cup dry white wine

6 cups chicken stock

¼ teaspoon freshly grated nutmeg

Salt

3 eggs, separated

6 slices whole wheat bread

1. Sweat the garlic in the olive oil in a soup pot over medium-low heat, stirring occasionally, until softened, about 3 minutes. Add the wine and reduce by half over medium-high heat. Add the stock, nutmeg, and salt to taste and bring to a boil.

2. Meanwhile, beat the egg yolks. Reduce the heat to medium-low, whisk in the egg yolks, and cook for 15 minutes. Cover and simmer for another 15 minutes. Adjust the seasonings.

3. Beat the egg whites (with a clean whisk) until stiff. Set aside. Place 1 slice of bread in each of 6 soup plates. Drop spoonfuls of the egg whites over the bread. Ladle the hot soup over the bread and serve immediately.

Note: Extra-virgin olive oil from Ganagobie Abbey is not currently available in the United States. You can substitute your favorite extra-virgin olive oil.

Brother Victor-Antoine d'Avila Latourette says this signature recipe from Provence is mouthwateringly good when it is made with olive oil from the monastery of Ganagobie. He makes this tapenade at his monastery in upstate New York, Our Lady of the Resurrection, and it quickly sells out at the local farmers' markets in Millbrook and Poughkeepsie. Locals often drop by the monastery to ask if there is any left! The tapenade is also available at the monastery's Christmas Fair.

Brother Victor's Serving Suggestions: Tapenade is typically used in France as an appetizer alongside an aperitif. It can be spread over crackers or slices of French baguette or eaten with raw vegetables. Tapenade can also substitute for a pesto in some pasta dishes, and it is used over fish in Provence. It's also delicious when mixed with a cooked egg yolk and used to fill the whites of a hard-boiled egg.

8 ounces (about 1½ cups) black pitted olives

15 basil leaves, shredded or cut small

6 medium cloves garlic, peeled

8 tablespoons extra-virgin olive oil from Ganagobie Abbey (see Note) or other
    young, fresh, fruity olive oil

2 tablespoons French cognac

2 teaspoons capers, drained

2 teaspoons fresh lemon juice

1 teaspoon Dijon mustard

1 teaspoon chopped fresh rosemary

1 teaspoon fresh thyme

Freshly ground black pepper

Place the olives, basil, garlic, oil, cognac, capers, lemon juice, mustard, rosemary, thyme, and pepper into a food processor and process until it turns into a smooth paste. Adjust the seasonings. Place the paste in a bowl, cover, and refrigerate until ready to be used.

Note: Extra-virgin olive oil from Ganagobie Abbey is not currently available in the United States. You can substitute your favorite extra-virgin olive oil.

TRUCCHIA
(Swiss Chard Omelet)

Serves 2

Brother Victor-Antoine kindly shared another classic recipe from the south of France—this one is for a tasty omelet that is made with Swiss chard. Trucchia is typically flat and thin and can be cut into 2 or more portions. Brother Victor says he usually serves the amount given here for 2 even portions, though he says the French sometimes cut it into smaller slices that are served as hors d'oeuvres.

Salt

1 bunch (6 leaves) Swiss chard, washed and trimmed, stems removed and
    reserved for another use, coarsely chopped

5 large eggs

Freshly ground black pepper

4 cloves garlic, crushed

3 to 4 tablespoons extra-virgin olive oil from Ganagobie Abbey (see Note)
    or other young, fresh, fruity olive oil

1. Bring a medium pot of salted water to a boil and blanch the chard until tender, 2 to 3 minutes. Drain thoroughly. When cool, grab a handful or two at a time, and squeeze the water from the chard; set aside.

2. Beat the eggs in a large bowl. Add the chard, season with salt and pepper, and mix well.

3. Heat the garlic in the olive oil in a 10-inch nonstick skillet over medium-high heat until the garlic is just starting to color. Remove the garlic and discard.

4. Add the egg–Swiss chard mixture to the skillet. Tilt the skillet in every direction so the mixture spreads evenly. Reduce the heat to medium-low, cover

the skillet, and cook for 2 to 3 minutes, until the omelet is set but the top is still moist.

5. Run a rubber spatula around the edge and bottom of the omelet to loosen it from the skillet. Shake the skillet to make sure no part is sticking. Wearing an oven mitt or using a towel to protect your hand and arm not holding the pan, place a large inverted plate over the omelet in the skillet. Quickly flip the skillet over so the omelet is on the right side of the plate. Return the pan to the heat and slide the omelet, browned side up, back into the pan. Continue cooking for a minute or two more until the omelet is done. Transfer the omelet to a serving plate and serve hot.

Note: Extra-virgin olive oil from Ganagobie Abbey is not currently available in the United States. You can substitute your favorite extra-virgin olive oil.

This salad is best served after a main course as a transition to dessert. In France it is often accompanied by a cheese plate. This recipe was adapted from Twelve Months of Monastery Salads *by Brother Victor-Antoine d'Avila-Latourrette.*

SALAD

1 head baby chicory (frisée), torn into bite-size pieces

1 bunch arugula, stems trimmed off

1 small bunch watercress, stems trimmed off and cut into bite-size pieces

1 Belgian endive, leaves separated and torn into bite-size pieces

VINAIGRETTE

¼ cup extra-virgin olive oil from Ganagobie Abbey (see Note) or other young, fresh, fruity olive oil

3 tablespoons Raspberry-Scented Vinegar (recipe follows) or store-bought raspberry vinegar

1 tablespoon Dijon, Meaux, or other French mustard

Salt and freshly ground black pepper to taste

¼ cup minced fresh chervil for garnish

1. Combine the salad greens in a good-size salad bowl. Toss until well mixed.

2. Just before serving, whisk together the vinaigrette ingredients in a measuring cup or a small bowl until thickened. Pour ¼ cup of the dressing over the salad and toss lightly until the greens are evenly coated. Add more as needed. Sprinkle with the chervil and serve immediately.

Note: Extra-virgin olive oil from Ganagobie Abbey is not currently available in the United States. You can substitute your favorite extra-virgin olive oil.

RASPBERRY-SCENTED VINEGAR   *Makes 3 cups*

3 cups white wine vinegar (see Note)

1 cup fresh raspberries

1 tablespoon rum

1. In a large pot, bring the vinegar to a boil over medium heat and continue to boil for about 3 minutes. Add the raspberries and rum, reduce the heat to low, and cook for about 2 minutes more. Turn off the heat. With the help of a masher, carefully crush the raspberries, then cover the pan and allow the vinegar to cool for at least 1 hour.

2. Pour the entire mixture into a clean, sterilized glass jar. A large canning jar is perfect for this. Refrigerate for 1 week.

3. After a week, pour the mixture through a fine-mesh sieve into a clean bottle, discarding the fruit. Store the bottle in a cool, dark place or the refrigerator.

Note: Brother Victor-Antoine d'Avila-Latourrette from Our Lady of the Resurrection Monastery near Millbrook, New York, makes white wine vinegars. They can be purchased in the abbey gift shop.

MONASTERY ETIQUETTE

DO consider a retreat even if you're not Catholic; monasteries welcome guests of all faiths.

DO practice silence as much as possible.

DO feel free to attend prayers. (It's polite to do so before meals.)

DO be on time for meals. Meals are silent and cleanup is a shared duty.

DO invite another guest for a walk if you both wish to speak.

DO bring flip-flops for the shower.

DO arrive before the abbey closes for the night, or you will be locked out.

DO bring cash or a check to pay for your room, because many guest-houses don't accept credit cards.

DO give more than the suggested room rate if you have the means.

DON'T be afraid to leave family and friends behind; the best retreats are spent in solitude and silence.

DON'T be nervous about attending prayers for the first time; sit in the back pews if you prefer.

DON'T sing along loudly; sing softly or follow the service in silence.

DON'T enter the monastic enclosure (where the monks and nuns live).

DON'T use cell phones on monastery grounds.

DON'T listen to loud music; use headphones.

DON'T speak after Grand Silence begins at night.

DON'T force yourself to attend Vigils; it's better to be rested
    in the morning.

DON'T ignore abbey instructions for cleaning your room
    before check-out.

ACKNOWLEDGMENTS

I am grateful to all the monks and nuns who welcomed me in the spirit of Saint Benedict. God bless you.

My parents awaited the completion of this book with the same mix of hope and anxiety with which they have greeted all of my journalistic endeavors. I couldn't have done it without them, especially my mother, who has always been my muse. To my dad, a professor emeritus of physics, whose mathematical skills I failed to inherit, I can only say thank you for patiently answering my amateur questions about the universe.

I am deeply thankful for the extraordinary friends who supported me through thick and thin. Angela Addario provided unflagging enthusiasm, expert research, and a profound familiarity with all things Catholic. Diana Weinhold offered constant encouragement and put a roof over my head in London, where I was able to write at the magnificent British Library. In New York, Pamela Gruen was a source of calm advice and offered financial support when I needed it most, while Doug Morris kept things in perspective with his famously dry sense of humor. Neill and Lynne Caldwell, Howard Cagle, Laurie Zoerb, and Hilary Short cheered me on, while Sandra Kim enthusiastically taste-tested monastery fruitcakes (she liked them all). Special thanks and all my love to my cousin Blair Muss in Manhattan.

The new friends I made while traveling have a special place in my heart, including Barbara Rodowicz, Sue Noble, Salena Troy, Marabeth Hobgood, Peter "Duke" DeLuca, Kelly Morgan, Marie Sferrazza, and Dr. Hans Busch. I'd also like to thank all the guests who shared retreats with me, especially Father Vincent Byaruhanga, Father John J. Yanas, Jr., Father James P. Whelan, Father William A. Mahon, Jr., Corinne Roberts, Susannah Marriner, Susan Chamblee, Elvine Gautier, Jacqueline Hue, Roselyne Fillonneau, and Iñigo de los Santos.

I am forever grateful to the priests, friends, and fellow worshippers who brought me into the Catholic faith through the Rite of Catholic Initiation for Adults (RCIA) at Saint Paul the Apostle in New York City. Father Bob deserves a special mention, as does Father Tim, who waded ankle-deep into the baptismal font with me.

Brother Gregory, a Christian Brother monk whom I met at the Abbey of Gethsemani, dusted off his French to write me a letter of introduction to the Christian Brothers in Paris; he remains one of my most treasured friends. I owe a special debt of gratitude to everyone who drove me to and from abbeys I might otherwise have missed: Brother Simeon of Gethsemani, Father Robert of Saint Joseph's, Renate Buchanan, Veronique Huyghe, Marcus Beirens, Rita Vermeltfoort, and Gumer Santos. I am also indebted to Deirdre Larkin at the Cloisters in New York for her erudite knowledge of horticulture and the Middle Ages.

Many thanks to all the chefs who contributed recipes. Every chef who took time out of a busy schedule to donate a recipe is a culinary hero in my eyes, but a few deserve special mention: Charlie Trotter and Rick Bayless in Chicago, Gray Kunz in New York, and Alain Solivérès in Paris. Thanks also to Dorothy Kalins and Melissa Hamilton for putting me in touch with my extraordinary recipe tester, Vivian Jao, without whom I could not have completed the book.

A very special thanks to my agent, Gary Heidt, who loved the idea for this project from the start and who took a chance on me, and to my editor, Sara Carder, at Tarcher, for her monastic patience and insightful guidance.

Glenn Wolff contributed illustrations that exceeded all my expectations and inspired me when exhaustion threatened to weaken my resolve. Thank you from the bottom of my heart.

Martine and François Varlet in Orleans, France, provided exceptional advice, maps, and contacts for the French abbeys and showed me the kind of hospitality I have only come to expect from monks and nuns. I could not have done the book without them, or without the support of monk and cookbook author extraordinaire Brother Victor-Antoine d'Avila-Latourrette. Special thanks also go to Will Keller, who helped me contact many of the American abbeys.

I'd also like to thank the dedicated (and sometimes fanatic) beer experts who gave me a crash course on Trappist beers: Tim Webb, author of *Good Beer Guide: Belgium*; Stu Stuart; Matt Dinges of the Shelton Brothers beer importers; and Sam Merritt and Jeff Wells, who treated me to a memorable Chimay tasting dinner. Cheese experts also deserve my thanks, including Laure Dubouloz and Hervé Mons in France, Steve Jenkins of Fairway Market in Manhattan, the staffs of the Ideal Cheese Shop in Manhattan and Bedford Cheese Shop in Brooklyn, and the cheesemongers for Whole Foods at Columbus Circle.

Two women provided comfortable rooms in their lovely bed-and-breakfasts at critical stages in the writing: Sally Baker of the Gold Coast Guest House in Chicago and Frau Decker in Rüdesheim, Germany. Kathy Daw kindly offered a quiet place to stay in Paris when my rented room in Belleville proved anything but contemplative. Thanks also to my Algerian, Pakistani, Bangladeshi, African, and Chinese neighbors in the Nineteenth Arrondissement, who, despite the noise, made it such a welcoming neighborhood.

SHOPPING GUIDE

If you want to make sure that one hundred percent of your purchase price goes to the monasteries, place your order with them directly (phone or e-mail is usually the best method for placing orders). Just be aware that the Christmas season is extremely busy and holiday orders must be placed early. Most monasteries offer their products year-round (except for products like cheese and chocolate, which can be difficult to ship during summer). There is a delicate balance between work and prayer in monasteries and most of them already do a brisk holiday business, so you can help them even out their work load by placing orders outside the holidays.

There is also a network of distributors, some monastic and some privately owned, who are dedicated to helping the abbeys reach a wider market, which is essential for their survival. The distributors listed below are all committed to ensuring the well-being and survival of the monasteries.

UNITED STATES

BEDFORD CHEESE SHOP

229 BEDFORD AVENUE (CORNER OF NORTH 4TH STREET)

BROOKLYN, NY 11211

888-484-3243

WWW.BEDFORDCHEESESHOP.COM

An old-fashioned cheese shop that stocks cheeses from around the world, including Trappist cheeses. Supplies vary, so check the website or call to see what's in stock. When the shop sells out of Trappist cheeses, the expert cheesemongers can help home cooks choose the right substitute for a recipe.

DEAN & DELUCA

WWW.DEANDELUCA.COM

Dean & DeLuca is an excellent source for gourmet ingredients such as candied chestnuts and extra-virgin olive oil, and for some Trappist cheeses. Supplies vary, so check the website or call to see what's in stock.

DEE VINE WINES

JOHN DADE THIERIOT

PIER 19, THE EMBARCADERO

SAN FRANCISCO, CA 94111

415-398-3838

WWW.DVW.COM

E-MAIL: DADE@DVW.COM

Dee Vine Wines specializes in German Reislings and carries a selection of wines from the Abbey of Saint Hildegard in Germany.

EBERHARD DISTRIBUTING, LLC.

DAVID EBERHARD

2035 SOUTH FILLMORE STREET

DENVER, CO 80210

303-757-5319

WWW.EBERHARDDISTRIBUTING.COM

DOCTORWINE@HOTMAIL.COM

This is another excellent source for wines from the Abbey of Saint Hildegard in Germany.

HEAVEN GOURMET
www.heavengourmet.com

Heaven Gourmet specializes in fine gourmet foods, coffees, and teas made by monasteries in the United States and Europe. It also offers gifts for cooks, including aprons, mugs, T-shirts, and cookbooks. Heaven Gourmet's mission is to create compassionate consumers while helping monasteries reach a wider market. A percentage of profits is used to help abbeys with special projects, such as building a new church.

IDEAL CHEESE SHOP LTD.

942 FIRST AVENUE (AT 52ND STREET)

NEW YORK, NY 10022

800-382-0109

WWW.IDEALCHEESE.COM

CHEESEINFO@IDEALCHEESE.COM

This award-winning cheese shop has been in business since 1954. It is a great source for cheese from the Abbey of Tamié in France and Chimay cheese from Scourmont Abbey in Belgium. The shop arranges deliveries anywhere in the fifty United States.

MERCHANT DU VIN

WWW.MERCHANTDUVIN.COM

Merchant du Vin imports some of the world's finest beers to the United States. Visit its website to find local distributors for Westmalle, Orval, and Rochefort beers.

MONASTERY GREETINGS

800-472-0425

WWW.MONASTERYGREETINGS.COM

Monastery Greetings specializes in religious gifts from more than one hundred Christian monasteries and hermitages, and also carries some food products made by abbeys. Customers can order online or call to request a mail-order catalog. It's an excellent source for Trappist Preserves from Saint Joseph's Abbey.

SHELTON BROTHERS

P.O. BOX 486

BELCHERTOWN, MA 01007

413-323-7790

WWW.SHELTONBROTHERS.COM

INFO@SHELTONBROTHERS.COM

Shelton Brothers imports some of the world's best beers and specializes in beers that are brewed in small batches using traditional methods. It imports Achel beers, and while you can't order directly, the company has a reliable network of distributors. Check its website for a distributor near you.

WHOLE FOODS MARKET

10 COLUMBUS CIRCLE

NEW YORK, NY 10019

212-823-9600

OR

250 7TH AVENUE (CHELSEA)

NEW YORK, NY 10001

212-924-5969

WWW.WHOLEFOODSMARKET.COM

The Columbus Circle cheese counter is an excellent source of information on all types of cheese and carries Chimay cheese from Scourmont Abbey in Belgium. The Chelsea store carries a wide selection of Trappist ales, including Orval, Rochefort, and Achel.

EUROPE

Note: For international calls, first dial 011 from the United States or 00 from Europe, then the country code, followed by the local phone number; if the local number begins with a zero, drop it when dialing from abroad.

AGAPE

WWW.AGAPE-ABBAYES.COM

Chambarand Abbey in Provence (a lovely abbey that no longer makes cheese but is still worth a visit) launched this site to help other monasteries reach a wider market. The website offers food and other products from more than thirty abbeys in Europe and Africa. The site is in French and some English. Fill out the online forms to ask a question, request a catalog, or place an order.

AI MONASTERI

CORSO RINASCIMENTO, 72

00186 ROME

ITALY

39 (0)6 6880 2783

WWW.AIMONASTERI.IT

Ai Monasteri carries products that represent Italian monasteries, but most of these are now made by commercial producers under licensing agreements with the abbeys. However, the artisanal jams and preserves from the Trappist nuns of Vitorchiano are still made entirely by the nuns;

these come in wonderful flavors like chestnut, cherry, fig, and grapefruit. Dr. Umberto Nardi's family has run the store for four generations. The English version of the website is difficult to understand in some areas.

L'ARTISANAT MONASTIQUE DE PARIS

68BIS AVENUE DENFERT ROCHEREAU

75014 PARIS

FRANCE

33 (0)1 43 35 15 76

WWW.ARTISANAT-MONASTIQUE.COM

ARTISANAT-MONASTIQUE-PARIS@LAPOSTE.NET

This is a collaborative effort by French monasteries to sell their products to the public in retail stores located throughout France. In addition to Paris, there are outlets in Lyons, Toulouse, Rennes, Nantes, Marseilles, Lille, and Bordeaux. Products vary by region. All sales support the monasteries. Contact the Paris store to learn more about other locations. Sales staff are volunteers, and most of them speak only French.

CAFÉ TRAPPISTEN WESTMALLE

ANTWERPSESTEENWEG 487

B-2390 WESTMALLE

BELGIUM

32 (0)3 312 05 02

WWW.TRAPPISTEN.BE

INFO@TRAPPISTEN.BE

This café, owned by the Trappist monks of Westmalle Abbey, lies directly across the road from the abbey. It serves cheese made by the monks from their own herd of cows, as well as the monastery's renowned ales. The café can be reached from Antwerp on the Antwerp–Turnhout bus route; public bus number 410 stops in front of the café.

MONASTIC ASSOCIATION

WWW.MONASTIC-EURO.ORG

Monastic is an association of more than two hundred Christian monastic communities that are located mostly in France but also in Germany, Belgium, Switzerland, Luxembourg, Italy, and Portugal. The association was created in part to protect the authentic identity of monastery products for retail and marketing purposes. Products are sold under the Monastic brand and are identified by the Monastic logo. The website is in French.

THE SPANISH TOUCH

888-480-0013 (IN U.S.)

34 93 555 57 15 (IN SPAIN)

WWW.THESPANISHTOUCH.COM

Elna Minguez offers personalized tours of Spain, including tours of Spanish convents in and around Seville that make traditional sweets. You can also sign up for her newsletter. The Spanish Touch is a member of the American Society of Travel Agents.

SUGGESTED READING

Architecture of Silence: Cistercian Abbeys of France, Terryl Kinder; photographs by David Heald (Harry N. Abrams).

Confessions of Saint Augustine, translated by John K. Ryan (Image Books).

Gethsemani Homilies, Matthew Kelty and William O. Paulsell (Franciscan Press).

In the Heart of the Desert: The Spirituality of the Desert Fathers and Mothers, John Chryssavgis (World Wisdom).

The Letters of Hildegard of Bingen, vol. 3, translated by Joseph L. Baird and Radd K. Ehrman (Oxford University Press).

A Place Apart: Monastic Prayer and Practice for Everyone, M. Basil Pennington (Liguori Publications).

The Rule of St. Benedict, edited by Timothy Fry (Vintage Books).

Saint Mary of Egypt: Three Medieval Lives in Verse (Cistercian Studies Series), translated by Ronald Pepin and Hugh Feiss (Liturgical Press).

The Sayings of the Desert Fathers, translated/introduced by Benedicta Ward, rev. ed. (Cistercian Publications).

Selected Writings of Hildegard of Bingen (Penguin Classics).

St. Bernard on the Love of God, translated by Terence Connolly (Newman Press).

Thoughts Matter: The Practice of the Spiritual Life, Mary Margaret Funk (Continuum International Publishing Group).

Cheese Primer, Steven Jenkins (Workman).

Flavors from Orval, Nicole Darchambeau (available in the Orval Abbey gift shop and at www.heavengourmet.com).

From a Monastery Kitchen: The Classic Natural Foods Cookbook, Brother Victor-Antoine d'Avila-Latourrette (Liguori/Triumph).

Good Beer Guide: Belgium, Tim Webb, 5th edition (CAMRA Books).

Rick Bayless's Mexican Kitchen: Capturing the Vibrant Flavors of a World-Class Cuisine, written with Deann Groen Bayless and Jeanmarie Brownson (Scribner).

Twelve Months of Monastery Salads, Brother Victor-Antoine d'Avila-Latourrette (Harvard Common Press).

Twelve Months of Monastery Soups, Brother Victor-Antoine d'Avila-Latourrette (Liguori/Triumph).

Westmalle Trappist: Met Eenvoudige En Lekkere Eenpansgerechten (Delicious One-Dish Meals Made Easy, with recipes in Dutch and French), Stefaan Couttenye and Jef van den Steen (Davidsfonds/Leuven).

Thomas Merton

No Man Is an Island (Harvest/HBJ Books).

Praying the Psalms (Liturgical Press).

The Seven Storey Mountain (Harvest Books; or any other edition).

The Sign of Jonas (Harvest Books).

Thich Nhat Hanh

Anger: Wisdom for Cooling the Flames (Riverhead).

Going Home: Jesus and Buddha as Brothers (Riverhead).

Living Buddha, Living Christ, 10th Anniversary Edition (Riverhead; or any edition).

Zen Keys: A Guide to Zen Practice (Three Leaves).

INDEX